MARK BEGO

COLUMBUS BOOKS
LONDON

To my partner in crime. . .
David Salidor:
'When *are* we going to make a living?'

First published in Great Britain in 1986 by
Columbus Books,
19-21 Ludgate Hill, London EC4M 7PD

Designed by Kirby-Sessions, London
Photos by Retna Photo, New York
Phototypeset by Falcon Graphic Art Ltd
Printed and bound in Great Britain by
R.J. Acford, Chichester, Sussex

ISBN 0 86287 301 0

C O N T E N T S

I N T R O D U C T I O N:
The Sade Dossier   5

A Smooth Operator   6
Sade's Childhood   21
A Design for Living   31
Entering the Diamond Life   43
Love Affair with Life   55
Fulfilling a Promise   67
Sade in Fashion   75
Living the Multi-platinum Life   87

D I S C O G R A P H Y   95

V I D E O G R A P H Y   100

F I L M O G R A P H Y   101

C H R O N O L O G Y   102

ABOUT THE AUTHOR

MARK BEGO is the author of four consecutive bestsellers: *Michael!* (1984) and *On the Road with Michael!* (1984) about Michael Jackson, *Madonna!* (1985), and *Rock Hudson: Public And Private* (1986). *Michael!*, which spent six weeks on the *New York Times* bestseller list and was translated into six languages, has sold over three million copies. *Publisher's Weekly* proclaimed *Michael!* 1984's top-selling biography.

Heralded in the press as 'the prince of pop music bios', Bego continues his reputation for predicting who's 'hot' in the world of international pop music with his ninth biography, *Sade* (1986). He is also author of *Julian Lennon!* (1986), *The Doobie Brothers* (1980), *The Captain & Tennille* (1977), and *Barry Manilow* (1977).

For two years Mark was Editor-in-Chief of *Modern Screen* magazine, and is the writer and editor of the anthology *The Best of Modern Screen* (Columbus, 1986), which contains classic Hollywood features from the 1930s to the 1950s together with a foreword by Debbie Reynolds.

Mark has frequently appeared on radio and television shows as an entertainment reporter and TV talk-show host. Over four and a half million copies of his books are in print.

A native of Detroit, Michigan, Mark Bego currently lives in New York City.

The author would like to thank the following people for their assistance in gathering information for this book: Bart Andrews, Rick Behnke, Michael Bradley, Randy Jones, Gino Falzarano, Chris Kingsley, Elliot Hubbard, Dede Miller, Susan Mittelkauf, Marie Morreale, Carolyn O'Connell, Nancy Parent, Jim Pinkston, Shelley Power, Sherry Robb, David Salidor, Tony Seidl, John Tobler, Walter at Retna Photo in New York and *The Sun* newspaper (London) for permission to reproduce its front page for 21 March 1986.

THE SADE DOSSIER

Full legal name: Helen Folasade Adu.
Known as: Sade.
Pronunciation: 'Shar-day'.
Birthplace: Ibadan, Nigeria.
Birthdate: 16 January 1959.
Ancestry: Nigerian/English.
Childhood: Clacton-on-Sea, Essex, England: 'Fifty per cent of the population were over sixty-five, the other half were poodles.'
Current occupation: Singing star extraordinaire.
Education: St Martin's School of Art, London. 'It was inevitable – I always knew I would leave home early.'
Work experience: 'When I started singing [four] years ago, I was trying to be a menswear designer.'
Other jobs: 'I did a little [fashion] modelling to support myself.'
Musicality: 'You could say that I'm a soul singer in approach.'
Musical influences: Billie Holiday, Smokey Robinson, Frank Sinatra, Bill Withers, Julie London.
Musical training: 'I just sing that way. It's not planned. It's not copied. It just comes out that way.'
Motivation: 'If you have this vision, this purpose, you can't let anyone get in the way and spoil it.'
Perception of fame: 'The trimmings don't impress me that much. What is nice about it is that the music we've made is

being appreciated and . . . that comes first. That means most to me.'
Creative associates: (1) Stuart Matthewman (sax and guitar); (2) Andrew Hale (keyboards); (3) Paul S. Denman (bass).
Name of band: Sade.
Original musical objective: 'My musical career was an accident.'
Goal as a group: 'We're creating our own sound.'
Description of compositions: 'Most of my lyrics are little stories about my experiences or those of my friends.'
Accomplishments: *Diamond Life* (album); *Promise* (album); *Absolute Beginners* (movie).
Awards: 'Best Album', 1985 British Phonographic Industry (BPI); 'Best New Artist', 1986 Grammy Awards (USA).
Spending: '. . . a ridiculous amount of money on clothes.'
Passions: 'Things that look timeless – just things that are classic and will last forever.'
Current residence: London.
Marital status: Single.
Dependants: A cat named Cylinder . . . 'She looks like a bat.'
Perception of public reaction: 'All the clichés of glamorous sophistication have little appeal to me.'
Fantasies: 'Do I want to live the British version of *Dynasty*? No thanks!'

5

A SMOOTH OPERATOR

The setting is a gilded art deco theatre in the middle of Manhattan, where the stage is artfully lit. The band makes its entrance and slides rhythmically into the jazzy introduction of the song 'Why Can't We Live Together?' Precisely on cue, she enters from the wings, appearing in the spotlight wearing an elaborately embroidered red jacket and tight black ski-pants. Her dark hair, slicked tightly to her head, is drawn back into a single long plait. Her eyes are almond-shaped, and her full and sensuous lips are glossed ruby red. As she opens her mouth to sing, the crowd at packed-out Radio City Music Hall, New York, swoons in ecstasy. They have been waiting for her. She has been dubbed 'the empress of cool' and 'the high priestess of understated sophistication'. She is the world's most alluring yet unassuming star . . . and her name is Sade.

SHE PERFORMS a sleek combination of jazz, pop and soul numbers, fronting the band that has adopted her name, Sade (pronounced 'Shar-day'), as its own. Her vocals are delivered smoothly and effortlessly, conjuring up hallucinations of the smoky nightspots of a long-gone era: a time of dimly-lit basement jazz clubs and soulful singers of the blues.

Unlike the legendary ladies to whom she is most often compared, Sade Adu is in no way mimicking the songs, style or performance of Billie Holiday, Julie London or Ella Fitzgerald. She is her own unique creation, with her own self-penned story-songs. As such, she has won well-deserved acclaim around the world. While her hit-making contemporaries like Madonna, Cyndi Lauper and Pat Benatar bare their souls for rock and roll, Sade has chosen to project herself with melodic, self-assured aplomb, floating above the jazz-like sounds of her band. Although she has been accused of trying to re-create the echoes of another era, Sade is instead re-defining the music of the 1980s.

She has said: 'I'm a big believer in things that last – books, buildings or songs. Like the Chrysler building, you know. Nobody says, "That's so ' 'thirties' " . . . it just looks good to generation after generation, and it will look good forever. There was nothing self-conscious about this "return-to-elegance" thing that I've been labelled with; it's just me. I don't wear spiky green and orange hair, because that's what *everyone* wears now, and I'd feel stupid in it. My music is understated. I like to get up in the morning and dress in a way that makes me feel confident. I like to listen to music that sounds as though it was made to last.'

Sade once studied to become a fashion designer, but she turned to a career in music and with her cool sound has created a musical trend to suit the world. She is heralded as the smoothest operator in the record business, and with her two multi-million-selling albums, *Diamond Life* and *Promise*, the Sade quartet has become the toast of six continents. From London to New York City to Tokyo to Sydney, the exotic sounds of Sade's hit singles 'Smooth Operator', 'Your Love Is King' and 'Sweetest Taboo' have topped the charts and made her into an international star overnight.

Sade was born in 1959 in Nigeria, to a Nigerian father and a British mother, and was brought up in Clacton, Essex. Perhaps it was not surprising that her sexy looks and fascination with creative expression should have attracted her initially to the London fashion scene. After studying at St Martin's School of Art, she designed and modelled clothes. Though she would not have been content to spend her whole life working with fabric, she did not realize when she auditioned as a singer for a band called Pride that the event would revolutionize her life. With the release of

the album *Diamond Life* in 1985, music fans of diverse tastes were immediately seduced by the jazz/pop sound of Sade and her band.

On 13 July 1985 she was one of the stars of the historic *Live Aid* concert, brainchild of Bob Geldof, and when she opened her sold-out début American concert tour in New York City's Radio City Music Hall she had the audience eating out of her well-manicured hand. On stage she has no need to rely on sequinned outfits, frantic gyrations or explosive special effects. She simply sings and sways to the music, mesmerizing her adoring fans with the texture of her voice and her exotic good looks.

According to Sade, 'People have criticized me for not

being dramatic enough on stage. I only do things that come naturally. Anyone can stick their arms out, dance around, pretend to cry. I'd feel embarrassed doing that. We try to preserve our dignity.'

Her creative collaboration with the three other members of the band, Stuart Matthewman (sax and guitar), Paul S. Denman (bass guitar) and Andrew Hale (keyboards), was immediate alchemy. However, Sade is the first to admit: 'I certainly never expected things to reach this scale.'

Indeed, in 1982 when Sade was expanding her career as a fashion designer, she had no idea of becoming a singing star. 'My musical career was an accident when I started singing four years ago,' she admitted in 1986. 'I was trying to be a menswear designer, and I did a little modelling to support myself. We all came out of the same nightclub scene in London. One day I was asked if I wanted to sing in a group, and I decided to try it. I have no technical training and am completely uneducated in music. In fact, I look at music more as a consumer than as a musician.'

A London group calling itself Pride needed a second singer, and one of the band-members thought that Sade might fit the bill. The audition went less than smoothly and Sade was turned down. However, two weeks later the players changed their mind and called to ask her if she could join them after all. When Pride eventually disbanded, Adu, Matthewman, Denman and Hale joined forces and adopted Sade's exotic name for the whole group.

Having once fancied herself as a writer, Sade found that she had quite a gift as a lyricist, and she began to furnish the words for the jazz-tinged music that her fellow band-members were busily crafting. 'I never had aspirations to become a singer until I was actually on stage singing,' she recalls, adding, 'I don't want to be a great acrobat or even be remembered necessarily as a great singer. I want to be considered more as a storyteller, a member of a regular group and a good songwriter.'

She is a diva devoid of ego. In fact the slightest suggestion that she should be labelled a 'rock star' is repellent to her. 'The mere notion is abhorrent,' she proclaims. 'If you're a rock star, then you can't be a human being. You can't invite your friends over to the kitchen and just communicate with them. I've got dear, dear friends that I've known for a long time, good friends who care every inch of the way. Those

friendships are important to me, especially when I have to put up with photographers climbing trees to take pictures of me at home or stalking the parks waiting for me to walk my dog.'

Like the majority of the pop and rock singers of the 1980s, Sade finds that making videos is an important aspect of her career. Her first video-cassette, the *Diamond Life* video, became a huge seller, making her the new darling of music television. In fact her work with video director Julien Temple led to her landing her first movie role, in Temple's full-length feature film *Absolute Beginners*. Will fame, success, money and stardom change the Sade that the world has fallen madly in love with? The lady denies the possibility. 'I'm me, just the same as me ten years ago,' she exclaims, 'and I plan to keep it that way.'

Just as the music on Sade's first two albums is easy-going, melodic and unpretentious, she maintains that the laid-back approach to recording the material on them was largely the key to its success: 'The way we approached making the album was in a way a bit naive. We just wrote it. It doesn't really apply to anything else. I guess that's partly why it stands out. It doesn't conform. *Diamond Life* has its own rules.

'I thought my songs wouldn't sit well in the charts. The band and I just wanted to make a good record, one that none of our friends would be ashamed of. It wasn't the fame that attracted us, it was the notion of having something on vinyl, a real record.

'Naturally, we were all over the moon about the success we achieved with *Diamond Life*, but we reached that status on our own terms. We made the album to our own specifications and musical standards. The fact that so many people shared those specifications was immensely satisfying to us all . . . and one hell of a bonus. We have never regarded, and will never regard, any music production as a business venture, and those who do are not true to their music or themselves. It's all to do with taste.'

Diamond Life sold over eight million copies worldwide, reaching the Top Ten in the album charts in Britain, Australia, Holland, France, Japan, Germany, Italy and the USA. In fact, in Holland *Diamond Life* outsold Michael Jackson's *Thriller*. Throughout Europe, the sweet sounds of 'Your Love Is King' and 'Smooth Operator' come wafting out of clubs and cafés, and photos of uniquely beautiful Sade peer forth from the covers of magazines such as *The Face, Number One* and *Cosmopolitan*. In America, *Time* magazine described her as 'grooving to a timeless talent', *Newsweek* found her 'sultry . . . elegant and serene', and *People* proclaimed her sounds 'seductive' and 'delicious'. In France, *Elle* magazine gave Sade the accolade of naming her one of 'the world's ten most elegant women'.

One of the reasons for Sade's overwhelming global appeal is the fact that she is impossible to place in any pre-existing category. No one can pin a label on her of the type that so often enables a performer to cross over to international stardom. Her music is neither soul, nor jazz, nor pop, but some sort of unique synthesis. And while she is gorgeous to look at, again she is impossible to categorize. She is neither black nor white nor mulatto in complexion, though her appearance has elements of all three. The shape of her eyes suggests an Oriental look as well. In reality, she seems to be a combination of the best features of every human race.

Sade claims to be glad that she doesn't fit neatly into any distinct category, in music or in life: 'I'm not really black, and I'm not really white. I'm a person with brown skin who was born in Nigeria and now lives in London.' The combination is enough to charm the entire world, it seems.

A massively successful début album is every recording artist's dream . . . one that hits the top the first time out. The traumatic part of instant success is plotting the course of the next album. After the amazing global appeal that *Diamond Life* had, could the formula be repeated? When Sade and the band returned to the record shops in November 1985 with *Promise* they proved that they were no 'one-hit wonders'. Britain, Australia, West Germany, Italy, Canada and Japan all jumped for a second helping of Sade, and in America the album *Promise* flew past Bruce Springsteen and Stevie Wonder to knock Barbra Streisand's *Broadway Album* off its perch on the no. 1 spot in the album charts. With a sold-out début American tour, the hit singles 'Sweetest Taboo' and 'Is It a Crime?' and a 'Best New Artist' Grammy Award, Sade lived up to the English translation of her abbreviated Nigerian name, which means 'crowning glory'.

While Madonna was busy playing sex kitten/pop tart, Whitney Houston was gaining appeal as a soul stylist *à la* Aretha Franklin and Cyndi Lauper was busy painting her hair and cavorting with moronic wrestlers,

Sade breezed on to the scene and presented the music world with what it unknowingly longed for: a breath of melodic fresh air.

According to Sade, one of the reasons that *Diamond Life* and *Promise* have such a relaxed and naturally appealing flow to them is that both albums are comprised of compositions that she and the band genuinely wanted to perform. There was never any pressure to create an album that was 'commercial' in any existing sense. Their music was something that they wanted to create, and if the public wanted to buy it, that would be a bonus.

'We never were businesslike,' explains Sade. 'We didn't think "money" or anything like that. We just wanted to make a record that our friends liked, that we were proud of, and we hoped that it would be a success. And in making the second album I never wanted to think, "Oh God, I hope this is as successful as *Diamond Life*!" I don't have great technical ability as a vocalist, although I always did think I could sing, sort of. I just sing a song the way I think it should be sung and that's it. I'm not a great acrobat and I'm no great technician. But I do feel that now I'm stretching a lot more.

'Perhaps in the beginning I wrote songs in a certain way because I was aware of the limitations of my ability. But I don't think anyone can turn to me and say that I've got a limited range any more.'

Although she is now the fastest-selling singing star of the 1980s, Sade has her feet planted firmly on the ground. She is an international star whose talents and beauty know no boundaries, yet she maintains that her success will never go to her head. Instead of running out and purchasing a Rolls-Royce, she prefers to make improvements to her beloved 1958 Wolseley. Instead of running around with a flashy group of culture-vultures who are impressed with her fame, she spends her time with the people who were her friends when she was still Helen Adu, the fashion student, and even retains some friends from childhood.

As she says, 'I refuse to take all this [her success] too seriously. I won't get too involved with it or care too much about it. It would make me crazy. I'd become obsessed with it, and that would be damaging because it would take so much time and energy and get me off a positive course. So I have to put this out of my mind and just hope for the best.'

On the other hand, Sade is not one to play safe. She

is not afraid of challenges, nor paralysed by fear of
what people will think. If it were not for her cavalier
attitude, she might never have moved from designing
fashion in clothes to creating fashion in music. 'I never
wanted to be a singer, even though I loved music. It was
more of a hobby,' she explains. Yet when the
opportunity to audition for Pride presented itself, she
welcomed the challenge of attempting something new.

'There are so many things that people can do that
they don't attempt; they think that they aren't clever
enough, that only So-and-So was cut out to be a
such-and-such. So many people are more talented than
they believe. You only have to believe in yourself and
try it. Don't be frightened of failing or looking a bit silly.
Anybody can try *anything*!' she declares, with confident
self-application.

It appears that it is Sade herself who is the 'smooth
operator' she sings about in her hit composition. Like
cream, she has risen effortlessly to the top. However,
even the most charming fairy-tales can include
unhappy plot twists. 'Everybody thinks I sail through life
and that I've had it easy,' Sade admits, referring to the
sugar-coating that her fans imagine overlies her
existence. 'I get amazingly great breaks; things happen
that most people only dream about, and then I'm
plagued by major setbacks, constantly.'

Sade's parents separated when she was three years
old; after that, half of her family lived on one continent,
the other half on another. For years Sade struggled to
bridge the emotional gap between herself and her
headstrong father who lived in Africa when she was
growing up in England. After the release and success
of her *Diamond Life* album, Sade was at last beginning
to get closer to him. Tragically, just as her second
album, *Promise*, was about to be released, her father
suddenly died.

Neither she nor the band-members had decided at
that point upon the title of the second record album. It
was early October, 1985, and a decision had to be
made. She recalls, 'My dad had written me a letter on
my 21st birthday. The day I heard of his death was the
day we had to submit a title for the album. I read
through the letter and there was a line in it that said,
"promise of hope".' After she had re-read his letter, the
word 'promise' echoed in her mind, and became the
obvious choice.

A mere four years ago it looked as though Sade Adu
was destined to establish her name as a designer of

men's fashions, competing with Giorgio Armani and Bill Blass. Having unexpectedly shifted career, she now finds herself mentioned in the same breath as Peggy Lee and Billie Holiday. It would appear that whatever field she had ultimately chosen, she was destined to reach the upper echelons.

Sade's life story began by spanning two worlds: England and Nigeria. In the short period of two years, Sade has conquered six continents with her voice, her beauty, her honesty, her introspective story-songs and her jazzy musical sophistication. Sade's love affair with life has just begun, and to her millions of fans around the world, her creativity is an inspiration.

S A D E ' S
C H I L D H O O D

The evocative British song stylist that the world has come to know as Sade was born on 16 January 1959 in Ibadan, Nigeria, near the Gulf of Guinea on the mid-western coast of Africa. The second child of an English mother, Anne Hayes, and a Nigerian father, Bisi Adu, she was named Helen Folasade Adu. The name 'Folasade' means 'crowning glory' in Nigerian, and it is commonly shortened to either 'Fola' or 'Sade'. From the time she was a baby, everyone referred to the little girl with the sparkling, warm brown eyes by the latter abbreviation.

IN THE LATE 1950s, London supported a good many smoke-filled basement clubs where rock and roll, and especially skiffle, was the great craze among the young. It was in London during this era that Sade's parents met. Her father was studying at the London School of Economics when he fell in love with an attractive young girl named Anne. They were married and had a son they named Banji. Soon afterwards they moved to Nigeria, where Sade's father had accepted a teaching job in Ibadan. Unfortunately, the marriage was not destined to last. 'My father was a very difficult man,' Sade declares.

In 1963 her parents separated. 'When I was three and a half, my mother left him,' she recalls. 'But I felt quite close to him in that I understood why he was like he was. My mother always taught us to love him. I think he's the only man she really loved.

'My parents' relationship had broken down to the point of no return, so my mother borrowed money from friends, did a moonlight flit to Lagos and came home. It was fairly hard to get out of Nigeria, especially for me because I was born there. My brother was all right because he had been born in England. We were on my mother's passport, so we were able to leave – although, in a sense, she should not have taken two Nigerian children away from their fatherland. It's not on. It's not cricket. She was lucky just to get away.'

Leaving the tropical weather of Nigeria for her grandparents' home in the Essex village of Great Hawkesley in the dead of winter was an awesome adventure for young Sade. 'We landed in England never having seen snow before, just shiny white sunshine,' she remembers. 'It was all just green and white, green and white everywhere.

'It was the worst winter in decades – bad luck, but I think when you're a child you just accept things like that. The thing that impressed me most, in fact, was the mole on my granny's face. She had an enormous mole on her face, and I think I was more taken aback by that fact than the snow and everything else.'

Sade also remembers the sensation of cold that the British winters introduced her to. 'My grandfather was a bit tight,' (meaning tight-fisted) she explains, 'and he wouldn't put heating in our room. We had icicles hanging from the condensation and ice along the inside of the window ledge. It was absolutely horrifying!

'From the age of three and a half I grew up in England,' she continues. 'Originally, we lived with my grandparents, who lived about 80 miles from London in a tiny village. My mother was doing nursing at the time so we lived there and my grandmother looked after us. When my mother completed her training she got a house given to her about four miles away from her job so we stayed there, but we were still out in the sticks until I was 11 and my mother remarried.'

Sade's mother adds, 'I was district nurse/midwife when Sade was a little girl. From [Sade's] age four to 12, we lived in West Bergholt, which is near Colchester. Because I was the district nurse we were very much part of the community. People there were very fond of Sade, and they still are.

'At school Sade was always very conscientious, but a bit of a rebel. She was very good at sport. She didn't have any strong ideas about what she wanted to do later. She was very artistic, very good at drawing. Her art teacher said she was the most gifted girl he ever taught. Her family's always been quite artistic, particularly on my father's side. I've still got paintings by my father's sister. I never really influenced what Sade would do. I've always felt that people find their own way. I've always encouraged Sade and Banji to do what they want. I don't believe in [saying,] "He will be a doctor," etc. Sade's always been independent, because quite a few of her relatives have been like that – fairly positive. I think the fact that she had only one parent made her more responsible.'

'SAY SADE'S NAME WITH CARE . . . IT'S PRONOUNCED "SHAR-DAY". YOU'LL BE USING IT MORE THAN ONCE!'

– *Seventeen*

It was not long before Sade was displaying her artistic flair in other ways, too. One of her early choices of creative expression was in the field of photography. Her mother explains, 'When Sade was younger she won the "runner-up" prize in a *Daily Telegraph* photo competition. The competition was on the theme "Places, People and Things". She did "People". That year we'd been to visit her grandmother in Nigeria and for the prize she had the photo [of her grandmother Adu] enlarged to about 15 inches by two foot. I've still got it hanging on my wall.'

Sade speaks with special pride when she remembers her grandmother Adu in Nigeria. 'My grandma is a herbal doctor,' she reveals. 'She makes herbal soap and sells it – and coral too (owning coral is a big status symbol) – to the kings in the surrounding territories. She's nearly 80, very determined and strong. She's a real character; she's got "Mama" tattooed across her chest. I've never met anyone like her. She makes me feel so proud! She bases a lot of what she does on mystical powers and spells. There's a great attitude when you get out into the country away from the cities.

23

People in the Nigerian villages are great. They're spiritual.'

One of Sade's first obsessions was to own her own horse. Anne Adu recalls what happened. 'Sade's very determined. Once she sets out to do something she keeps going. But I always say what you want isn't necessarily what's going to be best. For instance, when she was younger she wanted a horse. Unfortunately, when she eventually got it, it wasn't very suitable. It was a point-to-point horse, very delicate. She managed him and looked after him, but he practically ate us out of house and home. He had to go! Sade does think things out, but she has a certain naivety. She's a bit too optimistic.'

'Then, when I was 11,' Sade reflects, 'my mother remarried this mad butcher and we went to live by the coast, in Clacton-on-Sea. He was basically potty and gave a lot of entertainment to my friends . . . because he was so weird! Not long ago he was arrested as a peeping tom. That was well after they divorced. So all the nights he went off and she thought he was going off with another woman, he was probably peeping through people's windows.' She laughs.

'Clacton is a bit of a dead-end place,' explains Sade. 'It was not a great place for a young person, because 50 per cent of the population was over 65 . . . a rent-a-go-cart seaside town, full of poodles and old ladies. It is where the working-class people retire who have been there on holiday and liked it. They buy a house there for when they grow old. It's full of poodles and no poodle parlours. The only good things were the second-hand clothes you could buy there. Not a place for young people at all, and there were only three black people in the whole area.'

She remembers the period as a difficult one for the family, and is very proud of her mother having the courage to leave Sade's father in Nigeria to make a new life in another country. 'My mother struggled a hell of a lot. She was a white woman who had two brown children in the early 'sixties and came to England with one suitcase and nowhere to live. Nothing, really. I am fairly classless, because it is very difficult to class someone who comes from a mixed marriage. There isn't a class structure in Nigeria; there's a tribal structure and prestige as far as money is concerned. My mother comes from a family where her mother was very working-class and her father was middle-class stroke artsy-fartsy. My grandfather grew up in a

24

commune and my Aunty Phil still lives in one in Farmington, Connecticut.'

According to Anne Adu, 'The three of us – myself, Banji and Sade – have always been together. We've kept very close. Sade's got a granny and granddad in this country [England] who live about five miles from me. She's very fond of them, and of her grandmother in Nigeria, as they are of her. When I was doing my training her granny here used to look after Sade. She's really like a second mother. I think Sade has a very supportive family, which helps a lot. Even though there is no father, her family's very strong. It's important that people care about you – that's what matters.'

Sade describes her brother Banji as being 'as mad as a hatter' and 'a really talented furniture-designer. He's had lots of squats. He moves in somewhere, does it up brilliantly and then leaves it for somewhere else.'

'Sade hasn't changed a great deal,' her brother Banji proclaims. 'Neither has the relationship between us. When we were younger it was fairly classic older brother/younger sister – sometimes we'd get on well, sometimes we didn't. Sade was more interested in dressing-up then, and I was more into football. I don't think we've really become any closer over the years.'

Like so many teenagers, Sade began to escape from the boredom of her routine life into the fantasy world that music and records create. It was when she was 13 years old that she began to buy albums. Marvin Gaye, Aretha Franklin, Al Green, Billie Holiday, Van Morrison and Nina Simone were amongst her favourite recording artists. 'Anything soulful!' she exclaims. 'I've always had a passion and commitment to music as a consumer. Records I love make me completely happy, and I've always mixed with people like that, people who love music and get very precious about songs they've discovered. They're almost as musical as I am. If you enjoy something, you get involved with it.'

The music that she liked the most has left a lasting impression on her, and an influence on the music that she creates today. 'All the songs I've ever loved – even jazz stuff – are things that tell a story, like 'The Inflated Tear' [Roland Kirk], 'Sketches of Spain' [Miles Davis] – you feel you're in Spain! The soul stuff I like is Sly [Stone] and 'Family Affair' and Marvin Gaye, who always tells a simple story. It's all simple and unpretentious, and that's what music is to me. It should take you somewhere and move you in some way, and that's what I want our songs to do.'

Rock and roll, however, has never fascinated Sade. 'I don't think of rock and roll,' she explains. 'I never have. It's never played any part in my life at all. Then again, there are certain things, like Traffic, which might be classified as rock and roll, only because everything has to be pigeonholed and marketed. That Stevie Winwood's got a really great soulful voice. I don't say that I'm a Traffic fan, but there are some great soulful singers in rock and roll. So, I wouldn't say that I *only* like soul. I like good songs, but rock and roll in its purest form has never interested me.

'When I was 14, I looked for records. I went to bargain bins and secondhand shops, wherever. I don't know why I did; nobody told me to. But most people aren't even allowed to look any more. It has to be shiny and current and loud to be accepted, and it's a pity; it's really sad. Too many things are being missed by too many people because they aren't given the opportunity to hear it.'

Singing was not her reason for looking for particular records. 'No, it wasn't something I'd wanted to do since I was a kid,' she claims. 'I sang in the bathroom and with friends, just larking around, but I didn't ever think about being a singer. When I was younger I read all the music magazines and I was interested in the wonderful lives pop singers seemed to have, but that was about it. I was excited by music and it was a part of my life, but I'd never thought about doing it professionally.'

Her fascination with music and the world of singers was a great escape for her. It allowed her to forget about the awkwardness of her life as a teenager. 'My mum was always having car crashes. I remember once, I was completely squashed underneath all these bodies that had been sitting next to me!' she recalls. However, the most disturbing memory she retains from her early days is that of her mother's interest in the man Sade calls 'the mad butcher'.

'She wasn't a good-time girl,' says Sade of her mother, but it seems that Anne Adu found herself in a local social club '. . . where they learn to dance out to time to "My Sweet Lord" and "Chirpy Chirpy Cheep Cheep" and they get that "Whoopee!" Club 18-30 mentality!' It was there that Sade's mother met 'the mad butcher'.

'Obviously I was jealous,' Sade admits. 'My mother had never been with anyone. He had gout, six kids from a previous marriage and he reminded me of someone from *The Texas Chainsaw Massacre*. My mum isn't good at choosing men,' she concludes sadly. Somehow listening to Billie Holiday singing 'Violets for My Furs' was more fascinating than her mother's second marriage.

'HER LIPS ARE LUSCIOUS AND SHAPELY . . . BUT MOST SEDUCTIVE IS HER SMOKY CROONING VOICE.'

– *Playboy*

If Sade were stranded on a desert island and had to make a choice of the music she was to be abandoned with, many of her record album choices would be culled from her record-collecting days. On her list would be: Bill Withers' *Live at Carnegie Hall* ('Mine is all scratched, so I would insist on a new one. I wouldn't say Bill Withers is one of the greatest *singers* of all time, but he's definitely one of the greatest interpreters of songs ever'); Candi Staton's 'Young Hearts Run Free'; Nina Simone's 'Baltimore'; the Fatback Band's 'Wicky Wacky' ('One of the first things I ever danced to – it would take me back in time'); Roland Kirk's 'The Inflated Tear'; former-Temptation Dennis Edward's 'Don't Look Any Further' ('The best record that's come out as an American single for a long time. I didn't much like the rest of the LP, but that track is so summery and breezy, I love it!'); Marvin Gaye's 'What's Goin' On?'; Miles Davis' 'Sketches of Spain' ('That would take me to Spain if I wanted to go on holiday and couldn't get away!'); Sly and the Family Stone's 'Family Affair'; and of course a copy of *Billie Holiday's Greatest Hits* ('As long as it included "Strange Fruit", "You've Changed" and "God Bless the Child" ').

Her interest in records led to friendships with young people of her age who shared her fascination with jazz and soul music. 'We weren't trying to be rebels,' she says. 'We weren't making a statement. It's just that we all had a similar working-class background, and whatever we got didn't come easily. If anyone had a car or access to one, we shared it, shared the expense of driving 50 miles to find a decent club where we could dance. Nothing was put on a plate for us.

'I'm glad I haven't had an easy time,' says Sade of her years of growing up in rural England. 'I grew up quite quickly and quite young, and I understand people pretty well. I've learned to be tolerant and learned a lot from seeing disastrous relationships around me. It makes you stronger and makes you enjoy life more. I try to take people at face value, whatever they are. I try not to be frightened of people just because of what their label is, whatever paraphernalia they have surrounding them.'

According to Sade, 'If you really want something, you've got to get up in the morning and believe in yourself and believe in what you're doing. And that's not to say that some people are not born into situations that are much harder than [those of] other people. But the only way you're going to achieve anything is by having some belief in yourself.'

By the mid-1970s Sade had outgrown her quiet life on the Essex coast, with its poodles and blue-rinsed ladies. 'I wanted to do something I enjoyed, but which was at the same time creative,' she recalls of her need for self-discovery.

London beckoned, and Sade responded.

DESIGN FOR LIVING

Sade was 17 when she left home to attend school in London. She had already developed her own flair in the way she dressed, and she thought that the life of a fashion designer would suit her perfectly. She enrolled at St Martin's School of Art in the West End.

'I WAS THERE at an exciting time,' says Sade, looking back at the scene in London at the time, 'when punk fashions created a whole new fashion ideal. Music and clothes became totally interrelated. Although I have always thought of myself as a "soul girl", I really appreciated what the punk movement did for the design business.'

Although she liked the idea of becoming a fashion designer, the curriculum, the instructors and the teaching emphasis were not particularly to her liking. According to her, 'I got into it because I like to draw. I liked the creative part. But you really have to think about business first and foremost. I never liked that part of it. I don't miss it. I wouldn't go back to it, never in a million years.'

Her original concept of what studying fashion design was about appealed to her because it was a 'reasonably creative' and exciting career objective. However, she found out that there was much more to being a fashion designer than coming up with an outrageous idea for an outfit, drawing it and running it through a sewing machine. Cost, fabric texture and durability of cloth all have to be taken into consideration, as well as design.

'You have to be quite shrewd,' explains Sade. 'You don't design a garment that has certain vents in the back, because sewing those will cost more, and nobody's going to buy that kind of garment in a cheap fabric. You have to be a businesswoman before you're a creator, and I'm not. When you make songs, you don't have to think economics first – you just do it! But you have to have the same feeling of self-confidence, especially when you have nothing behind you in the way of experience. If you didn't, you wouldn't even get out of bed in the morning.'

Although she was still interested in designing menswear for a living, she was not particularly enthralled with the study of the craft. 'It was a badly designed design course,' she laments. 'The tutors were living in Cloud Cuckoo Land and knew nothing about real life.'

Sade soon found out that one cannot be taught to be artistic. 'Either you can or you can't, and most people come out of college not knowing any more than when they went in. If only they geared it to the technical side more, people would get jobs. There are lots of people doing one thing who would be better off doing something else.' It was the creativity that fascinated her, not the mechanics. 'I wanted to immerse myself in the painter's life,' she sighs. Still, she forged ahead with her studies, amassing her own distinctively designed line of menswear.

People who saw Sade's designs were impressed with the young girl's fashion sense. Her clothing designs soon led to her first move from fashion to the world of music. In the spring of 1981 a fashion show was to be held in New York City in conjunction with a performance by the British band Spandau Ballet. The fashion display was known as the Axiom Show, and the work of two aspiring London designers was selected for it.

One of the most significant results of her voyage to New York City was the fact that Sade became acquainted with three people who were destined to become her lifelong friends. First there was Melissa Caplan, who was a fellow designer from St Martin's School of Art. Then there was Rhonda Paster, who was later to become Sade's personal assistant when she switched to a singing career. And last, but not least, she met the journalist Robert Elms, who wrote for the British magazine *The Face* and who became Sade's long-time boyfriend.

'I first met Sade in New York,' Melissa recalls. 'We were both at college in London at the same time. Although we didn't know each other, we knew *of* each other. Someone who worked with both of us said to Sade: "I've never known anyone to swear as much as you except Melissa Caplan!" ' She laughs.

'When we did meet,' Melissa continues, 'I think we were both expecting an argument, being rival designers. But she was too exhausted from the flight and I was too busy, so we both felt sorry for each other and got on instantly. Sade thinks details are very important. She has to get things exactly right. She gives herself too much work, but I understand it.'

Rhonda Paster remembers, 'I first met Sade when she was designing clothes. She came out to New York with Spandau in 1981 and she ended up staying at my ex-husband's house. Sade was exactly the same then as she is now – but poorer! She hasn't changed in looks, although she's got nicer clothes now. She never mentioned singing though – never. That's why it came as such a surprise.'

Robert Elms remembers distinctly the day he met Sade. 'I was in New York with Spandau for the Axiom Show in May '81, and I knew these two girl clothes-designers were coming over. I walked into Rhonda's one day, where I was staying, and Sade was standing in the middle of the living room. Honestly, my first thought was, "Thank God they've got a good-looking model!" – 'cause we were recruiting models then. After that it turned out that I pulled her, amid a lot of competition from Gary Kemp and others! The thing was, I'd never been aware of Sade at home, because she wasn't really a nightclub girl. She had her own friends and she'd prefer going to the pictures or whatever.

'Sade's a great one for not knowing who the hell you are. She didn't know who Pete Townshend [of The Who] was when he phoned up once. Literally didn't! So when I told her I was Robert Elms from *The Face* – showing off – she hadn't heard of me. Soon after that I moved in with her,' he reveals.

He continues the story: 'As a clothes-designer, Sade was struggling then, but she was really, really good. Mainly menswear. Just as you'd expect of her, very understated, good fabrics. The sort of things she's always appreciated. But she started rowing with the people she was working with and she jacked it in. Sade does like to row! She also started modelling. She hated modelling. She hated modelling with more passion than I've ever known anyone to hate a job.'

Sade herself describes the task of modelling as 'the worst job known to man. I used to do anything to get out of it, it was so boring!' On the subject of boredom, Sade was finding the fashion scene not to be as exciting as it was cracked up to be. She found herself longing to 'work on a boat and read books'. This, however, was a pipedream rather than a serious career objective – not least because of her need for some financial security: 'I knew there was a limit to how long I'd be willing to dig in the couch for loose change whenever I wanted to buy cigarettes.'

For a time, Sade contemplated becoming a novelist. She had an interest in writing, and fancied herself as an author of sexy, feminist-angled books about women in control of their destinies, and of their love affairs. If Erica Jong, Barbara Cartland and Jackie Collins could do it, then why not add Sade Adu to the list? Erica Jong's *Fear of Flying* had made an inspirational impression on her, so she decided to give it a go. 'I'd just bought a couple of her books, and I thought, "I could do that!" ' Sade recalls.

'SEXY, JAZZY, SOIGNÉE, ORIGINAL, GORGEOUS, EXOTIC, FRESH, INSPIRING, COOL, COMPASSIONATE, CLASSY: SADE!'

– Mark Bego

Robert Elms remembers, 'Sade wrote a brilliant series of short stories for a thesis at college. They were all on love. One was a parody of a sex book, one of Barbara Cartland's . . . that was a funny interlude! At one stage she decided she'd write books like *Fear of Flying* and become a millionairess. She went and bought two of those books, read them and was about to do it. . .' but another opportunity presented itself, an opportunity that Sade had never once seriously considered – singing.

At the time, Sade was working in the evenings as a waitress to earn money, and wondering to herself, 'When am I going to make a living?' Fate was about to serve her a new entrée on her career menu, quite by chance.

As Sade explains, 'I was going to design college in London and we went around to all the clubs to see the fashions. We got to know a lot of people and in this little club I met this bloke Lee Barrett, who asked if I could sing. I was feeling very cocky, so I replied that I probably could. I knew he was involved with a band, so I thought he was just having fun with me. "You look like you probably could," he says. "Why not try out with my band?"

'He figured maybe I'd be all right because I was tinted.' (Sade laughs at the idea some people have that all coloured people can sing.) 'I thought about it for thirty seconds, then said, "Yes!" After working hard all day, I needed a distraction in the evenings,' she explains, adding, 'When singing came up, I didn't think about making a career of it. I don't do crocheting and I don't play badminton, so I thought, "This could be a good hobby."

'It was a funk bank called Pride, and they wanted a back-up singer,' Sade remembers. The audition session turned out less satisfactory than planned. 'I was just thrown in at the deep end and asked to sing harmonies. I was told to come in and out, meant to be some sort of genius computer brain and remember what I was supposed to be doing. Basically, I failed. I was very shocked. Lee came back and said, "I'm sorry, but they don't think you're suitable."

'I had never been turned down for anything,' she recalls, still stunned by the memory of the rejection. 'It hadn't even crossed my mind that they might not want me! I suppose I sounded pretty dreadful. It was a bit of a disappointment, but I didn't care all that much. They thought they'd find somebody better for sure.' Oddly enough, the members of Pride couldn't find anyone better suited for the position, 'and two weeks later they came back to me and said, "We cannot find anybody. We need you!"

'They'd changed their minds, so I thought I'd do it to help them out,' she continues. 'I thought, "Why not? I'm not proud." So I joined the band. Everybody was just struggling to get a group together, to get some sort of recognition and, ultimately, a record deal.'

As she had had no vocal training, Sade had to dive in

and follow her own intuition over how she sang. 'I just had to learn how to harmonize. There are certain things you can't be taught anyway. Technique you can be taught, no doubt improving your ability. You can be taught to improve what you've got. You can't actually be taught how to sing.'

Pride had been through a couple of major changes. At one time the band had been called Ariva. The addition of Sade marked its transition from Ariva to Pride. The person in the group with whom Sade Adu was supposed to harmonize was a girl named Barbara Robinson, who was the band's lead singer. Barbara recalls, 'The first time I met Sade was when I was in Ariva. Lee [Barrett] said, "How do you feel about singing with another girl?" I wasn't into that idea. I was getting quite used to singing on my own! So she came down and sang, and I thought, "Well, she's not brilliant. . ." There was nothing then compared to the voice there is now. But, once we started together in Pride, the voices blended so well: mine being the high one, hers the husky. We worked out all the harmonies together. Sade's got a very good ear for that.'

According to Barbara, 'Sade was always the one who knew exactly what was going on. She really knew what she was doing. She always had a say in the songs, while I didn't because I can't write to save my life. All I wanted to do was sing. I think she always set her sights higher than just being a singer in a band, but her set certainly wasn't planned from the beginning. At first we were both treading very carefully.'

The band was not making any money at this stage. It was really little more than a hobby for its members. Her urgent need for cash put Sade once again in front of the camera, modelling designers' clothes. She sums up her feelings about fashion modelling as follows: 'I've just never been interested in it that much. I've done some modelling, but I haven't had any romantic assignments in exotic regions of the world. I've just done boring in-house stuff, nothing major. I just did it to make ends meet. With the money I made, I could live more comfortably than the rest of the band!'

It was while she was part of the group Pride that she began wearing her hair in the distinctive style that she most often adopts: pulled back, away from her face, with a long plait cascading down her back. 'When I was with Pride, I had my hair really long,' she remembers, 'and the guitarist was constantly swinging his guitar around. One night my hair got caught on his guitar, and I was moving everywhere he went. He wasn't even aware of it. He was the only one in the entire club who wasn't!'

Pride evolved further when a saxophone player named Stuart Matthewman joined the band. It was not long before he ushered in two of his musician friends, a bass-player named Paul S. Denman and a drummer whose name was also Paul . . . Paul Cooke.

What was happening was that within the group two separate bands were emerging. There was Pride, which had Barbara as the lead singer and Sade Adu singing harmony vocals, and there was a second group with Sade in the forefront. Pride was more funk-based in sound, while Sade's solo outings were becoming a bit more jazzy in approach.

According to Sade, 'Stuart had a lot of song ideas apart from what we were doing with Pride, but we had our energies invested in Pride, so anything apart from that came together slowly. After a while we got to playing with this drummer Paul, and we worked up a short set: a few favourite covers, including the Julie London classic "Cry Me a River", and a couple of things we'd worked out called "Cherry Pie" and "Hang on to Your Love". Both of them are on the album [*Diamond Life*], but at the time they were written, a record was nowhere in sight.

'Once I started writing with Stuart,' she continues, 'it was easy because we had the same attitude about the kind of music we wanted to make. Of course, the playing had to be high-quality and the tone of it was a mature music with a commitment to soul.'

So divergent were the styles of Pride and the Sade-led ensemble that someone in the group came up with the idea of having Sade, Stuart and the two Pauls open the show, then, after an intermission, the full Pride band on stage. This formula was tested out one fateful night at Ronnie Scott's club in Soho. The opening act performed cover versions of 'Why Can't We Live Together?', 'Be Thankful for What You've Got' and 'Cry Me a River', plus their own compositions – 'Cherry Pie', 'Hang on to Your Love', and another song they had put together called 'Smooth Operator'. Because they didn't have a name for themselves, it was decided that they would take the nickname of their lead singer Helen Folasade Adu and call themselves 'Sade'. According to Sade herself, the decision wasn't made because she was fronting the band, but because 'it seemed an unusual name for a band at the time'.

Their appearance that night at Scott's was very important for Sade and her two groups, so even her mother, Anne Adu, came down to London to catch the act. She has vivid recollections of that evening: 'I saw her the first time she sang solo at Ronnie Scott's. I was very impressed. The thing was, I didn't know she was singing on her own. I went along to see her group Pride, so when I got there I didn't know what was happening. At first the boys came on and Sade didn't appear. She had troubles with her dress.'

True to form, fashion designer Sade had chosen an outfit that was destined to make an impression. Unfortunately, her dress that night almost ruined her début solo singing performance.

Sade says of the evening in question: 'We did a showcase at Ronnie Scott's, the jazz club. It was mostly friends there and a lot of record-company people trying to decide what they were going to waste their precious money on. The band went on and started doing Timmy Thomas' "Why Can't We Live Together?", the idea being that I come on after their intro. Unfortunately, the new dress I'd got for the big occasion was a bit tricky to get on, so by the time I was all together, the song had finished. I think the boys thought I'd run away. So they came off and we started all over again!'

By this point, Sade had learned not to become fazed by on-stage mishaps. At the beginning, she had had some uncomfortable moments: 'The first time I performed, it was awful. We débuted in this small club and there were cracks between the boards on the stage. At one point, I got my heels caught in a crack. I spent the rest of the set leaning forward to sing into the mike and trying to maintain my balance.'

Well, needless to say, the band that called itself 'Sade' was a smash at Ronnie Scott's. That was the beginning of the star we know as Sade, and the beginning of the end for the band known as Pride.

Peter Powell, a DJ on BBC Radio One, was the first DJ to present Sade on the radio. 'I first saw Sade when they were part of Pride,' he remembers. 'It was all very conceptual and perhaps too sophisticated for the time. Certainly, I think the two-band idea – to keep Pride *and* Sade going at the same time – was destined for disaster. Even then Sade [Adu] was a complete star, as was her rhythm section. I remember their songs were very long when I went down and saw them in rehearsal. They were beautiful songs, but very intense. I saw Sade when she sang at the Royal Festival Hall and she was dramatic and brilliant. But there's still a lot of room for improvement, which is the exciting thing about her. At the moment she's good, but she will turn out to be excellent.'

Eventually, Paul the drummer dropped out of the 'Sade' quartet and a keyboard player named Andrew Hale completed the foursome. The group continued to be a part of Pride, but was striving for a musical identity apart from the larger ten-piece ensemble. According to Sade Adu, 'We just wanted to make real songs that aren't full of catchy gimmicks like fast food. A real song is something that moves you in some way.'

The group Pride made it across the Atlantic Ocean to do a one-time-only gig at New York City's rock club Danceteria, but Sade Adu's development as a performing artist was already paving the way for its demise. She was becoming caught up in the whole music-as-a-career idea. As she explains, 'The lead guitarist, Stuart Matthewman, and I started to write together. He'd show me a song, and I would tell him what I thought, change melodies and chorus lines. I broke down the mystique of being a songwriter, and that gave me a bit of confidence. At the same time I kept designing – it never occurred to me that you could make singing a career. It just happened. Singing began to take over my life. I got so much enjoyment out of it, I wanted to do it all the time. I grew to love it so much. After a while I knew it was the career I wanted.'

It was basically the record companies and their offers to the 'Sade' quartet that spelled the end for Pride. 'We were offered deals practically from Day One,' says Sade. 'Nobody wanted Pride. They only wanted the small group. In the end Pride just said, "Go on and take the deal." '

Of course there were a couple of offers from record companies who wanted to own the group's publishing rights on their compositions, so the right deal had to be acquired. At this time the four members of the Sade band were drawing unemployment benefit – the grand sum of £25 a week.

As Sade herself attests, 'Our dream was to make a record of our music. We wanted to make records as a group and stick together as a group and enjoy it. Nothing can come between that – and you mustn't let anything come between that.'

What the band needed was a couple of samples of their songs, recorded, mixed and presented to the record companies in the proper professional fashion. Enter record-producer Robin Millar. Sade describes what happened: 'We met Robin through a mutual friend of ours, Simon Booth, who was familiar with the project, and thought Robin would be perfect for it. He's a very stylish producer. He likes to work with layers of instruments, but subtly, so that we still sound like a four-piece. Ours is an intimate sound, and we didn't want someone that would bury it in too much embellishment.

'HELEN FOLASADE ADU IS ... THE SLEEKEST ACT TO ARRIVE THIS YEAR . . . A GARBO FOR THE M-TV ERA!'

– *Hollywood Reporter*

'Look,' she continues, 'a producer's job is to bring out the best in you. If Robin felt he had to use harmonies or emphasize the bass in spots, or any of those things . . . he knows what he's doing and if that's what it takes to bring out the best in the music, then what's wrong with that? The songs weren't written to showcase me, they're written for the band Sade to perform. I'm another instrument in the band. Everyone involved had a lot of input, and so did Robin.'

The band enlisted their old friend, the other Paul (Cooke), on drums, and went into the studio to produce two completed tracks that defined the sound that the band Sade was all about. They came out with the cuts 'Smooth Operator' and 'Your Love Is King' and soon afterwards clinched a deal with Epic Records in London (Portrait/Epic in the USA). The band called Sade was well on its way. The deal was signed in October of 1983. The less lucrative offers were declined ('Six points and £60 advance aren't much good to anybody!' Sade sarcastically noted). The Epic deal was for an advance of £60,000 plus 14¾ per cent of record sales. Yet the band could have had no idea of how much money it was about to amass, once the public heard the resulting LP.

The group that called itself Pride is now history. Barbara Robinson is working on a theatrical singing career and the other musicians have scattered. According to Barbara, 'It'd be silly to say I couldn't care less when the group split up, but there you are – all good things come to an end. We still see each other when we can, and at least something good came out of it. Of course, when she [Sade] does interviews now, Pride gets more mentions than [it did] when we were all together!'

According to Sade, 'It wasn't like this big breakaway. We even supported Pride, and we were encouraged by everyone in the band. Ultimately, the rest of Pride said, "Go and take the deal." That's what we did.'

At this point – late 1983 to early 1984 – Sade, Stuart, Alan and Paul had their greatest challenge ahead of them: creating a whole album to encompass the brilliant, smoky jazz-club feeling that they produced so successfully on stage: as Sade puts it, 'good music with a sort of timelessness to it, music that will be around in 20 years'. They went into the Power Plant recording studio (in Willesden, north-west London) with several creative thoughts and ideas as to the best way to achieve the album they envisaged. They returned with a masterpiece.

ENTERING THE
DIAMOND LIFE

Two years before, she had been enmeshed in designing clothes and selecting the appropriate fabrics for wear and fashionability. Suddenly Sade Adu had shifted career gears and found herself on a new course, one which was not of her own design.

HERE SHE WAS, a relative novice in a recording studio with three young-but-experienced musicians, ready to create their first record album. Whatever Sade might have lacked in musical experience she certainly made up for in intuitive feeling and expression. All art is creative expression that communicates something to others, whether it is a painting, a hand-made suit or a song. Sade had always displayed great sensitivity and sophistication. As the lyricist and solo vocalist for the band bearing her name she instantly became its undisputed focal point, setting the tone for its repertoire and its direction.

For Sade, style and feeling have always outweighed other considerations. She has said: 'I care more about the songs than the way I sing them. The most important thing to me is the lyrics.'

She has never felt the need or the desire to imitate anyone else. She was clearly her own creation, almost oblivious to media fads and consumer trends. 'The music is the most important thing. That is what ultimately justifies any direction people might push us in. I don't ever want to sell out or do what is expected of me. I want to keep improving on what we have, rather than change as things around us change. I don't think hit songs come from formula. I think formula comes together almost accidentally from the way you work together as a band,' she proclaims confidently.

The *Diamond Life* album was hand-sewn by the band, stitched together from the heart, as though it were a fine garment. Of her brief career in the fashion industry, Sade has said: 'I designed menswear. I liked using wool and cashmere. I don't like wacky clothes.' She applied the same aesthetic to her music.

Robert Elms recalls: 'From the start, Sade was going to be the one who dictated what the songs were like. And Stuart didn't challenge that. It was accepted it would be Sade's taste. That's what it's always been, all along – that Sade's taste is right. As a clothes-designer, photographer, cook . . . I think that confidence comes from her being an outsider – being half-black, half-white, being someone strange in Clacton, coming from a broken home, just being not like the people around her. Sade's always relied on her own taste rather than judging [things] on somebody else's.'

The album ultimately mirrored Sade's own uncomplicated attitude to life. 'That's the way I tend to approach things,' she admits. 'I'm not over the top. I'm not wacky. I'm fairly understated, and that reflects in the way I sing. I don't necessarily think that you have to scream and shout to move somebody. Sometimes I am screaming and shouting: to me, I'm really putting something in and really saying something. But when it comes out the other end and people hear it, they think it sounds very understated. Maybe at the right time, with the right song, I *will* belt and I *will* go over the top, but I don't think that to overstate is the best way of putting something across.

'The same applies to everything,' she continues, 'to clothes and design and architecture. It's now so acceptable to be wacky and have hair that goes in 101 directions in several colours, and trendy, wacky clothes have become so acceptable that they're . . . conventional. From being at art college, I've always hated people that have the gall to think that they're being incredibly different when they're doing something in a very acceptable way, something safe that they've seen someone else doing. I don't look particularly wacky. I don't like looking outrageous. I don't want to look like everybody else.'

When people initially heard cuts from the *Diamond Life* album, everyone from members of the public to reviewers to DJs began categorizing the sound as a

brilliant new form of jazz. Indeed, jazz was the major influence on Sade's three musical partners, affecting both their delivery and their style.

A truly talented musician, Stuart Matthewman had begun his musical training at the age of six. His first instrument was the clarinet. At college he studied music theory, and it was there that he began to play tenor saxophone. Sonny Rollins became his jazz idol. Stuart played with several unsuccessful pop groups and eventually landed a gig touring around Europe in the band of an Elvis Presley-imitator named Rupert. After leaving Rupert's act in Stockholm, he returned to London and joined Pride. His favourite musicians include John Coltrane, Gato Barbieri, Isaac Hayes and Quincy Jones.

Andrew Hale grew up in Wembley. A student of English literature at Sussex University, he worked as a nightclub DJ in Brighton. He joined Sade's band in 1983 equipped with his Wurlitzer and his ambition-driven talent. A self-proclaimed 'soul boy', Andrew is into bop and ballads, soul and salsa music. His strong taste for jazz is embodied in the music of trumpet-player Chet Baker.

'HIGH-GLOSS GOOD LOOKS!'
— *Rolling Stone*

Paul Spencer Denman is from Hull, Yorkshire. He moved to London in 1980, and he and his bass floated from gig to gig without his having a firm career direction. In 1982 he was invited by his friend Andrew to come to one of Pride's rehearsals. The rest is history. Paul likes the jazz sounds of Jaco Pastorius, Ron Carter, Charles Mingus and Charlie Haden.

Since Sade Adu most closely follows the music of Dinah Washington, Frank Sinatra, Marvin Gaye, Bill Withers, Nina Simone, Smokey Robinson, Ray Charles, Joni Mitchell, Tom Waits and Billie Holiday, she proclaims that her own vocal approach is derived from pop, filtered through her image of herself as a purveyor of emotional story-songs.

'I wouldn't call myself a jazz singer, because I'm not. I'm not trying to be. There's a jazzy feeling in there, but

46

it's one that I probably notice less than other people. In fact, when I first started being interviewed and people mentioned jazz, it wasn't even a term that I associated with us. Good music is good music, and I can't really intellectualize a lot about it. Sometimes jazz and soul make me feel the same way, because music is for making moods, making you feel something. Both jazz and soul play a part, have a role. But there is a massive difference in the ways jazz and soul are structured,' she says. She has described her music as 'moody and, I think, fairly emotional. . . I don't know if emotion comes across but I feel it does. It's fairly soulful, and it's just got a jazz colouring. I mean it's not in any way improvised jazz, it just has that colouring in the way I phrase and the way the sax-player phrases.'

Regardless of whatever label anyone wanted to put on it, the album that the band Sade recorded in 1983-4 was unlike anything else in the record charts . . . Michael Jackson was *the* international musical media sensation of 1984, swiftly followed by Prince. Bruce Springsteen, after ten years of roller-coasting degrees of success, was emerging as a major star. Cyndi Lauper, swathed in garish junk-shop outfits and with multi-colour painted hair, was telling the world that 'Girls Just Wanna Have Fun'. With rags tied in her blonde-streaked hair, a multitude of black rubber bracelets encircling her arms, crucifixes around her neck and a well-exposed navel, Madonna was climbing her way to pop-tart stardom. Hard-as-nails Tina Turner was making the comeback of the decade with her proclamation-of-survival LP *Private Dancer*, and those legs that just wouldn't stop. Now a cool breath of fresh air was about to blow through the world's music scene: an unknown girl and her band whose name was Sade.

From the first echoing bongo-beats of 'Smooth Operator', you know that you are in for something soothing yet exciting. Paul's bass comes up from below, and Stuart's moody sax is clear, melodic and strong. Sade Adu's voice, husky and all-knowing, joins them with her spoken narrative about an opportunistic cad who breaks hearts from LA to Chicago. Her voice is lush and low as she shifts smoothly from speaking to singing. Suddenly you feel that you are sitting in a dimly lit jazz club. The sound is dreamy and lulling, bitter-sweet yet effervescent. Sade's own heart is obviously one of the ones this smooth operator has broken. The song weaves an indelible spell. It is a melancholy ode for anyone who has loved and lost. Sade's voice neither competes with nor leads the band: it is an emotionally expressive instrument.

Sade composed 'Smooth Operator', her first foray as a lyricist, with Pride's guitarist Ray St John. They originally wrote the song together so that Sade would have a solo singing spot in Pride's stage show. It has gone on to become her signature song, as well as an apt description of Sade herself – the woman who charmed the world with her beauty and her voice.

'Your Love Is King' was written by Sade and Stuart two days before they were due to go into the studio to cut their pre-Epic demo tape. Stuart reveals, 'We never write the same way twice. What happens is that Sade will have some words which may suddenly fit to something. I'm strumming on the guitar. But with "Your Love Is King", the tune and words just popped into her head one day.'

Set at a slightly lower tempo than that of 'Smooth Operator', 'Your Love Is King' is a simple ode to love, with Sade's husky voice and Stuart's sax in the spotlight. The ballad is an uncomplicated expression of emotional obsession, with the type of instrumental interplay that shows off the quartet as a strongly unified troupe.

'Hang on to Your Love' is a peppy, more pop-oriented number, giving Stuart the chance to play guitar rather than sax, while Paul's bass work is predominant. On the instrumental bridge of the song Andrew's keyboards also shine on this Adu/ Matthewman composition.

'Frankie's First Affair' finds Sade returning to the story-song formula, giving lyrical advice to a lovelorn friend, while the band provides her with a languid bossa-nova beat. The song is simple, direct and very appealing.

'When Am I Going to Make a Living?' is an anthem for the 'me' generation. The lyrics of the song came to Sade when she was trudging home from the bus-stop one night in the pouring rain. As the thoughts came to her, she jotted them down on the back of the only piece of paper she had . . . an unpaid bill. Sade's sudden *a capella* last line concludes the song's message brilliantly with her clipped yet defiant 'hungry but we're gonna win'.

She is at her most soulful on the delicious 'Cherry Pie'. Paul's heavy, thumping bass line sets a mood reminiscent of the best of Motown. Sade's fluid singing dazzles throughout this funky guitar-layered sizzler. Credited to all four members of the band – the only Adu/Matthewman/Hale/Denman composition on the LP – the song has a looser vocal line and some attractive instrumental work.

'Sally' is the album's torch song extraordinaire. From the first low notes of Stuart's sax to the end of Sade's sardonic vocal lament, it is *Diamond Life*'s one sapphire, a precious gem with a hauntingly blue tint. Sade's singing is at its 'mood indigo' zenith. The lyrics deal with depression: 'I got the idea for that song the last time I was in New York, waiting for a bus on Bowery and 3rd Street, outside the Salvation Army. There were a lot of homeless young men outside. Sally was the mother figure, or the prostitute, welcoming people, giving them a place, "doing our dirty work".'

The song 'I Will Be Your Friend' displays the warmth of Sade's controlled contralto. She gets so intimate with the microphone, you can hear her draw breath. Jazzy, bopping and percussion-laden, the song shows off the tight interaction between the band's instrumentation and Sade's distinctive voice.

The album ends with the Timmy Thomas composition 'Why Can't We Live Together?' Although far more successful in execution than the original 1972 soul hit, Sade modestly tries to play down the idea of doing other people's material. She explains, 'The only reason we included that particular track on the first album was because it had always been featured in our stage shows and was part of the group's make-up. However, in most cases I believe that classic songs shouldn't be interfered with too much. After all, the reason they are classics is usually the fact that someone has recorded the ultimate version which could never be bettered – so why try?'

Happily the band tried – and succeeded. Despite Sade's trouble with her tricky dress the first time the band performed this number, the song is still used to open their concert act with a bang. Beginning with keyboard, bongos and bass, it is an apt anthem of racial harmony – and a song that allows Sade to belt a bit. Seductively to-the-point, it also makes one hope that she will make another exception to her rule about not recording other people's material and put on disc her interpretation of 'Cry Me a River' before too long.

For some strange reason, record companies like to tease consumers by including additional cuts on the cassette versions of their artist's albums. On the

European cassette version of *Diamond Life*, two such collector's items are included in the package. 'Snake Bite', an instrumental number by Stuart, Andrew and Paul, is edited on to the end of 'Smooth Operator' without a break. However, this is not the same instrumental extension that is used on the video version of 'Smooth Operator'. And at the end of the same European cassette 'Why Can't We Live Together?' is followed by the slow and beautifully torchy ballad 'Love Affair with Life', written by Sade Adu and Ray St John. In the USA, 'Love Affair with Life' is the flip side to the single of 'Your Love Is King'.

As for the album's title, *Diamond Life*, Sade has commented: 'It's not very easy to find a name for an album. ['Diamond'] means something that sparkles with a hard edge that has a lot of planes and sides to it. If you have a life like that, you can't go wrong. It's hard, but it's got such sparkle to it.'

With the exception of 'Smooth Operator', 'Cherry Pie' and 'Why Can't We Live Together?', all the songs on *Diamond Life* have lyrics by Sade Adu and music by Adu and Matthewman. According to Stuart, 'Writing with Sade is the most manic job in the world, because you'll just start to do something in her flat and the phone will ring. Sade can never just sit down. She has to be up cleaning the cat tray or looking at photos for a session. In a way I wish we could sit down, but it seems that most of our best songs are written in a manic rush. I wouldn't say she's very patient with me. We have some marvellous fights. When we were just starting on songs for *Diamond Life*, we had one massive argument over some song or other and I stormed out of the flat. Just as I was going out the door she caught me on the back of the neck with an acoustic guitar. We ended up writing the rest of the album on a guitar with only five strings! Actually I thinks it's a bit of a compliment that she tends to take it out on me. It's much better than bottling it all up.

'Spontaneity is very important for us,' he continues. 'We write the song first, just sitting around with the guitar with no thought of the production. Most of today's music is written around the production. It's boring to know exactly where the strings will come in and hear the same guitar sounds in every record.'

Explaining Robin Millar's role in the execution of *Diamond Life*, Stuart comments, 'Robin's job is to capture our sound on tape. The spaces are important. That way you can hear everything rather than filling it up with lavish production. The sound is basically sparse.'

According to Sade, 'Every band hopes to get a deal with a major company, but when it actually happened for us my initial reaction was, "I'm scared! Can I do this?" I don't have mike fright or anything, but the whole idea of recording. . . You think it's what you want, but it doesn't always turn out how you imagine it will. If I had been on my own, I would have had a hard time going through with it, but I had a responsibility to the band. It's a very stressful process, the anxiety of doing your tracks by yourself . . . and after a while you don't know how well you're doing any more. Then you don't know what the record is going to sound like because you haven't heard everybody's parts. Then before the final mix you go through it all over again because you don't know what that's going to sound like. I'm not really a high-strung person, but the recording process, especially the first time, will make a basket case out of anybody!'

Total artistic control is what every creative person would ideally like to obtain, whether they make records, films or books. It can also be very frightening on the first occasion when such control is given . . . suddenly all of the responsibility belongs to the artist, as does the credit if it is a success or the blame if it is a failure.

'SADE ADU IS LIKE HER SONGS – SMOOTH, ELEGANT AND BEAUTIFULLY ARRANGED.'

– Spin

'It was obvious that we were capable of making music without record-company intervention,' says Sade of the experience. 'The British company didn't even change the original order of the tracks.'

Not only were her expressive vocal performances up for public scrutiny, but her compositions as well. As she says, 'Anybody can shove a few romantic lines together and make them seem deep and profound. In fact, it's

far harder writing a song that is just coherent and straightforward and honest.'

Sade, Stuart, Alan and Paul had no idea how their creation was going to be received by the record company or by the public. The record company was enthusiastic about the product; its only concerns were to give it the right packaging and the appropriate marketing. The distinctive *Diamond Life* album cover was designed by Graham Smith, the photographs were by Chris Roberts and Sade Adu's make-up for the cover shot was done by Paul Gobal.

Sade knew Graham Smith already; he describes their association: 'The first work I did for her was a couple of photo sessions when she was with Pride, and then a poster for her first live performance at Ronnie Scott's. My first sleeve for her was "When Am I Going to Make a Living?" [the single]. I decided the artwork should be simple, stylish, nothing too gimmicky – similar to her own clothing, which has that classic simplicity. We looked at a lot of the old Blue Note jazz covers done by a guy called Reid Miles, and decided we wanted to keep all the sleeves for *Diamond Life* and the singles along that same jazzy line. The only trouble was that the record company was never too impressed with those, because they were black-and-white photographs. They wanted to promote her as a high-fashion glamour girl with slick airbrushed sleeves. So there were a few rows about that to start with, but Sade always had her way.'

When *Diamond Life* was first released in England in the summer of 1984, no one could have known what record-buyers were going to think of this début album. And still less did Sade know that she was soon going to have the whole world at her feet, heralding her as the saviour of the 1980s music scene. *Diamond Life* found its audience, and Sade discovered the perfect setting for her blossoming creativity.

LOVE AFFAIR
WITH LIFE

In February of 1984, Epic Records in England released the group Sade's first single, 'Your Love Is King', which made a healthy showing in the charts. It was followed by the equally appealing 'When Am I Going to Make a Living?' By August of that year, the *Diamond Life* album was no. 2 in the British charts and was also in the Top Ten in the Netherlands. The band's career had gone from 'Hang on to Your Love' to 'hang on to your hats'!

A DELIGHTFULLY ASTONISHED Sade Adu commented, 'I was surprised at the speed at which it picked up and the acceptance of the audience, because our music is so much our sound, our feeling, and it doesn't necessarily fit comfortably with the chart music. I was amazed at the speed at which people took to it. I think everybody in a band, every musician, is aiming for that, but I thought it would take maybe two or three albums before people fully understood or got a feeling for what we were doing.'

Such was not the case with Sade. Not only did the music on the *Diamond Life* album appear to be just what the public had been waiting for, but once the press got a look at the *distinguée* Ms Adu, she was an immediate star. Within a year her almond eyes and lush ruby red lips had graced 17 international magazine covers. The critics flipped for the girl, the band and the mystique that was 'Sade'.

Gushed London's *Record Mirror*, 'All she has to do is stand there. . . That she sings is a bonus. And sing she does . . . she's taut, restrained, but never icy or distant. At once she's haughty and unobtainable, then the girl-next-door. A star!'

Although she professed not to be a jazz artist, and that her band was not a jazz band, Sade found herself in July 1984 on stage at the prestigious Montreux Jazz Festival in Switzerland, where the crowds went crazy for her. 'It was Friday the 13th,' she recalls. 'Absolutely everything went wrong. We got to the airport late and missed a flight and had to take a helicopter to another airport, and when we finally arrived they weren't going to let me into the country. I had to leave my bags, clothing, everything at the airport. I am fairly superstitious. I mean, I *never* go into the auditorium and look at the stage from the audience's point of view. I think I'll always have stage nerves. I think I've got a long way to go as a performer anyway, but even when I've reached my height, I don't think I'll stop being nervous. Luckily, we got on stage at midnight, and it had become the 14th, so everything went smoothly. I got a letter from the director of the festival saying it was "magic". That's the biggest compliment we've ever been paid.'

Taking the show on the international road was an important part of making Sade's début album such a success. She claims that touring with the band is much more fun than going on holiday on her own. 'I much more enjoy going somewhere with the band. It's always funnier. You know, the more people, the more disasters that can happen,' says Sade. According to her, everyone in the troupe shares the responsibility. 'No one would enjoy it if one person was truly the boss,' she explains. 'It's like when you go on holiday with someone who is incredibly messy, you will take the responsibility to keep the place tidy. That's the way it is with the group. Somebody decides they are going to be the responsible one for the day. I'm not aware of what exactly it is, but we have a system and everybody pulls their weight.

'Tokyo was the most exotic,' says Sade, telling more tales of the road, 'but Rotterdam is such a depressing place. We stayed in the worst hotel I've ever been in. It was pretending to be high and mighty when in actual fact it was just a guest house with a clever little charade going on around it. I would rather have a little lady with a cigarette hanging out of her mouth saying, "No men in your rooms and you have to be in by nine'' than the sort of thing that went on in this hotel. You would order a cup of tea and it would arrive four hours later with a thick film on top of it, and if you asked to have your shirt cleaned and pressed it would come back looking – "yuck!" – like most of Rotterdam had driven over it!

'I've been in so many other countries, I'm neglecting my home town. But it's been very exciting. I would say it's fairly hectic and exhausting at times, but I guess I've enjoyed it, and the most important thing is that I'm a good buddy with the rest of the band. We have many laughs, and maybe not in such a funny situation sometimes, but, you know, we get on well and it's fun,' she concludes.

When *Diamond Life* started selling into the millions, Sade modestly quipped, 'My family must be buying lots of copies!' However, she was quick to announce, in typically cool fashion, 'Fame isn't important to me. What does mean a lot to me is the opinion of people whom I respect. If fame is important to the people I respect, then, yes, I want it!'

Life had suddenly become a succession of photo sessions, personal appearances and press interviews – a glamorous existence. But there was still one more major nut to crack: North America. Although she was the new darling of Europe, the United States and Canada were virtually unaware of the soignée charms of Sade. February of 1985 was scheduled for the audio assault on America, because that was when *Diamond Life* was due for release on that side of the Atlantic.

Before 1984 ended, however, it seemed that December would be the appropriate time for the band to 'chill-out' in a tropical climate and regenerate its energy. And so the quartet packed its bags and headed for Sri Lanka.

As Stuart Matthewman later explained, 'We tried going to Sri Lanka . . . to write songs. The idea was we'd sit on the beach with just a guitar, a Walkman and some blank tapes and write. But you can't. Not with sea and sun and all that. In the end we had to lock ourselves in our hotel room for a couple of days to write anything.'

Sade recounts one of her adventures in Sri Lanka aboard a 30-foot yacht: 'It was so sleek, if you coughed it ended up on another island. With no land in sight, the yacht was 90 degrees to the water, the boom was going crazy and the only efficient sailor on board was pissed out of his head and being sick in the bottom of the boat.

People started drowning next to me and I had no choice but to attempt to save them. If I'd had any sense I would have swum on. It sounds like an exaggeration, but it really happens. I thrive on disaster and adventure. It keeps me on my toes.'

Diamond Life hit the American charts in February, 1985; by May it hud sold a million copies, and was well on its way to selling a second million. Likewise, the single 'Smooth Operator' had hit the American Top Ten and Sade Adu was the media's darling . . . on her own terms.

At the American headquarters of CBS Records, which owns Epic and Portrait Records, the executives decided that the best way to market her in the States was to present her as the next Diana Ross. Wrong. Sade would have no part of it, and from that point on all of her publicity was handled by her personal publicist. She wanted to be presented on her own terms, and the ploy was intuitively on-target.

Rave reviews for Sade and her *Diamond Life* album from the American and Canadian press came in by the dozen:

'Stunningly photogenic, Sade possesses a dusky, haunting pop-jazz alto whose blasé sensuality perfectly matches her sleek appearance.'

Stephen Holden, *The New York Times*

'The entire *Diamond Life* album is a triumph of identity-building for Sade . . . even without seeing how stunning Adu looks, she commands attention on vinyl. Her husky, breathy tone conveys easy intimacy and elegance.'

Brian Chin, *Record*

'Not since Astrud Gilberto walked "The Girl from Ipanema" on to the beach of our heart twenty years ago has a husky voice so beguiled listeners with its promise of exotic, bitter-sweet amours.'

Ariel Swartley, *Vanity Fair*

'Her vocals, softly syncopated with a jazzy flavor, come upon you quietly, then suddenly deliver a knockout punch. Her style, simultaneously cool and warm, radiates great charm.'

Seventeen

'The bass drops languid R&B licks against a guitar that shifts mid-bar from a bossa to a hint of Philly soul . . . welcome to the international cocktail hour.'

Carol Cooper, *Village Voice*

'Sade's music establishes a seemlessly urbane mood that suggests late-afternoon champagne, if not Campari . . . the latest sensation from England.'

Robert K. Oermann, *USA Today*

'Sade seems to have found her ideal sound . . . her music is all pop-jazz finesse . . . wonderfully redolent of black cocktail dresses, scotch on the rocks and slow-dancing till dawn.'

Christopher Connelly, *Rolling Stone*

The international cocktail hour indeed! Whether Campari, scotch or champagne was the drink in question, there was no question but that Sade was suddenly the toast of the continent.

However, relations with the American record company were rather strained, especially when it discovered that Sade did not fit into a neat little pre-formed mould. She was a beautiful brown girl who was neither Donna Summer nor Billie Holiday. Yes, she was half 'pop' and half jazz in sound, but they soon found out that she was 100-per-cent her own creation. No duets with Julio Iglesias, please!

This conflict all came to a head in March, 1985, at the CBS Grand Convention held in Honolulu, Hawaii. Everyone wanted to see what this exotic new bird from Britain was all about. 'There was a sense of paranoia,' says Sade, describing the experience. 'Everyone wanted to have a look and say, "Oh yeah, that's the new one." It was like being the new girl in the class. It was very peculiar to be surrounded by people who you know are really watching you. It was very much like being a goldfish. We were there to expose our talent to the company who were going to put energy and enthusiasm behind us practically. That was the idea. The whole experience was like being in McDonald's . . . you know what you want, and you know what you're going to get.

'We'd be sitting on the beach,' continues Sade, 'and you could see them approaching with "manager" shorts on – bermudas with turn-ups, very clean, no ice-cream spilt on them. You can always tell because they have to appear as if "success-reflects-in-the-way-you-dress" and all those other mottos they use.'

Sade got a bit tired of being treated like merchandise at a china sale. 'I was very aware of what our role was. We were there to be used. But I intend not to be manipulated. You can avoid that if you're fighting, driving at it. I honestly don't think the music business is any different from any other business. It's maybe slightly less efficient, because you've always got to deal with a personality. That's obviously a problem to the record company – that the actual artists are a bit of a spanner in the works. There's nothing they can do if someone turns around once everything's smooth and planned and says that they don't want to do it. If it was any other product – a washing-up liquid, say – it would remain consistent to its behaviour. It would always be green and liquid. But every now and then somebody does a star turn.'

Another case of mistaken imagery came on a television show in Europe. Sade and the band like to keep things simple and clean. When they arrived on this particular set in Brussels, they found that it was designed to look like a night at the Moulin Rouge. 'We were on this show which had this hideous pink backdrop and steps leading down into an audience in dinner-jackets and bow-ties being served cocktails by waitresses – really sophisticated. And the director was trying to get me to go down among them and walk. It was all supposed to be very "dreamy". We got very depressed in the dressing-room because we started to think: "Is that what people really think we're like?" '

When Sade initially came to the United States to promote *Diamond Life*, she was quoted as saying, 'Making it here is very important to me. I've always loved American music. I grew up listening to it and I think it's been my biggest influence.'

Speaking of the initial success that she had in the beginning of 1985 in America, Sade remembers that 'Initially, it was the black stations who gave all the support, and the main reason for that support – or so we've been told by countless DJs in the States – is that the album brought a "breath of fresh air" to the scene. None of the stations could put us in any convenient category, which was convenient in that black station support was then followed by across-the-board pop airplay.

'If we had attempted to utilize a deliberate commercial format when we recorded the album, I don't think the term "breath of fresh air" would have been in any way applicable . . . we would have been regarded, and quite rightly so, as pale imitators of so many others. Let's face it, America has more than enough artists willing to do that, so why bother with "imports" of the species?' she asks.

What finally happened was fantastic: Sade's records were not only topping the pop charts, but they were also topping the black charts, the easy-listening charts and the jazz charts.

Privacy had now become a problem. Before the album topped the British charts and sold over six million copies worldwide, Sade lived anonymously in north London, in a former fire station. She had lived there for three years, paying only £6 a week in rent. In early 1985 she moved into a third-floor apartment in Highbury, overlooking a park, where she created her own environment: 'I've got a cactus against one wall and there are lots of shadows and shapes.' Although Robert Elms originally moved into the apartment with her, he afterwards found his own flat. (Sade said of his move, to Bloomsbury, 'He's always wanted to be part of the Bloomsbury set. I have my place and he has his.') Sade now shares her home with her friend/assistant Rhonda Paster and her cat Cylinder.

As soon as she settled into her new place, an anxious German photographer climbed up into a large tree across the street from Sade's windows, hoping to snap some candid pictures. Unfortunately for him, he lost his footing in the old horse-chestnut, breaking his arm when he fell from his perch. The local authorities then pruned the tree's lower branches to avoid a re-run of the episode.

If any situation becomes a real hassle, Sade has

been known to use the phrase 'more nerve-wracking than *Live Aid*', referring to the international concert event that she and the band took part in on 13 July 1985.

The show, which was viewed by one and a half billion people around the globe, was of course produced to raise money for the starving people of Ethiopia. Seventeen hours in duration, it was broadcast live via satellite from Wembley Stadium in London and JFK Stadium in Philadelphia and featured a roster of international performers which read like the *Who's Who* of the rock and pop world. There in the middle of all of it was the band Sade, performing for the largest audience for any show in history.

The acts performing in Philadelphia included Madonna, the Beach Boys, the Four Tops, Joan Baez, Hall & Oates, Mick Jagger, Tina Turner, Patti LaBelle and the Pretenders, to name but a few. At the British end were Paul McCartney, Elton John, Phil Collins, Alison Moyet, Queen and, amongst several other stars, Sade.

Prior to the event, Sade admitted that she was very excited about being part of it, '. . . not so much for the number of stars appearing, but for the amount of results we can get from it really. I'm optimistic that a lot of money will be raised. I'm realistic about the fact that in cases like this, not everything does arrive [in terms of food reaching its intended destination], but one per cent is [still] better than no per cent.'

Was the Live Aid event especially significant to Sade since she was born in Africa? 'Not really,' she reflected. 'I was brought up to have compassion and care about people who aren't necessarily as fortunate as myself, and therefore I think it's more compassion than feeling any more a kindredness . . . I just care for people irrespective of what race they are, if they need help.'

Sade's set at Live Aid was very tight and effortless-looking, and brought a welcome change of pace from those of some of the flamboyant rock artists who were on the bill. There was Sade Adu in a figure-hugging white high-collared top, similar to a turtleneck, and a black embroidered jacket over it. She wore black pants, huge gold hoop earrings, and of course her hair was in its signature plait. The first number the band performed was 'Why Can't We Live Together?', a perfect 'message' song for the event. Sade next swung into the hit single 'Your Love Is King', much to the excitement of the crowd. She removed her black jacket with a great flourish, to reveal that the top she was wearing was backless. She looked cool and stunning throughout the set. The third song she sang was the début of 'Is It a Crime?' from the *Promise* album that the group was working on at the time.

The show was a great showcase for Sade, because it introduced the group to such a huge global audience. 'The image is one of the main selling points,' says Sade's manager Lee Barrett. He is quick to point out that the band's first American single, 'Hang on to Your Love', was not a hit in the States, because there was no visual image of the singer. 'The American fashion world is acutely aware of what happens in Europe, and Sade has been featured in several American fashion magazines, including *Vanity Fair*. Naturally the American music business also watches European trends very carefully, seeing what works in marketing terms and what doesn't, before launching an artist in the US.' And of course, Sade's performance at the Live Aid concert helped to feed the hungry as well as spreading awareness of the group.

July 1985 saw the début of Sade's *Diamond Life* video-casette. Containing four video clips from the *Diamond Life* album, the *Diamond Life* video (CBS/Fox Video) became a huge hit, and leapt into the Top Ten music video-cassette sales charts.

The video version of 'Hang on to Your Love' takes place in a gambling casino, where we see a man betting. He loses his money. Sade and the band are performing on stage at the same casino, and footage of them is interspersed throughout. The gambling man looks into his wallet for additional funds, and we see a photo of his wife and baby. As his thoughts turn to them, we cut to his wife at home, dancing on point with the baby in her arms. The husband is obviously going to gamble away the rent money. The video is very stylized. The Sade band is seen playing very cartoonish cardboard musical instruments, reminiscent of the style of illustration of jazz album covers of the late 1950s. The clip was directed by B. Ward and K. Thorton, in a *film noir* style.

'Smooth Operator', which was directed by Julien Temple, opens with Sade being interrogated about her manager in a police station. As the music starts and the song get under way, we see Sade on stage in a nightclub. Her manager is also her lover, and she finds out in the course of the action of the video that not only is he two-timing her with a waitress in the same nightclub but he is wanted by the police for his shady dealings. It is he who is the cad, the 'Smooth Operator' that Sade sings of in the song. He has been smuggling weapons and breaking hearts. Finally there is a chase scene on a fire-escape in which Sade Adu's life is saved by the cops . . . in the nick of time.

'Your Love Is King' was also directed by Julien Temple. It is especially sparse and very stylized in the manner of the early 1960s. In it, Sade wears all black, including a pair of wrist-length leather gloves. It is intercut with footage of Sade dressed in white and performing card tricks in which the kings always seem to appear. There are lots of delicious facial close-ups of Sade, and some good shots of her fronting the band.

'When Am I Going to Make a Living?' is set in the present, with Sade wandering around London, asking the question of the song title. There are some great shots of the Sade quartet sitting together in a booth at a pub, having a drink and a few laughs. Directed by Stuart Orme, the video is very straightforward, with some cleverly intercut footage.

Each of the four music videos is preceded by a short monologue from Sade Adu, who talks about herself, her background and her life as a singer. All in all, the *Diamond Life* video is a well-conceived and entertaining package.

Since the group had experienced such huge international success subsequent to the July 1984 British release of the *Diamond Life* album, its next big challenge would be the follow-up LP. Sade said at the time, 'I want to make a record that proves to people that we *have* got something. Everybody's very skeptical about someone who has early, huge success. I want to prove to myself that there's something there. We've only just started, and we've got a lot to do. *Diamond Life* has been a success, but that's finished now. We're only just getting used to working together as a band; I'm just getting used to singing. I've had a lot of exposure at a point where I'm only just learning, only just teething. Obviously people expect an awful lot because of the amount of reaction we've had, but I feel a lot more confident now about songwriting and singing, even though I've still got a long way to go. I want to make a great album to follow *Diamond Life*, so we can stretch and come forward as a band.'

Sade is a lady who keeps her promises.

F U L F I L L I N G
A   P R O M I S E

The *Diamond Life* album had made Sade Adu an overnight media sensation. However, instant stardom is often followed by instant obscurity. The accident of being in the right place at the right time with the right sound has created many music-industry celebrities who hit it big with one album and then faded into the background. Try as she might, Carole King could never top her 1971 *Tapestry* LP, which is still the best-selling album by a female vocalist. After Peter Frampton broke records with the sales of his 1976 *Frampton Comes Alive* LP, his career took an immediate nosedive. Could the group Sade recapture the magic that made *Diamond Life* sparkle? The answer was excitingly affirmative.

COMMENTING ON the acclaimed 'smoothness' of the *Diamond Life* album, Sade Adu has said: 'It may sound smooth, but there are a lot of mistakes. I shouldn't say "mistakes". Rather, there are things we could improve on. Then again, by improving on it you could refine the thing too much. To me, it sounds very uncultivated. To someone else it might sound smooth, but that feeling sort of came naturally to the group. It isn't outrageously inventive or original, but it's fresh for the times, and it's outside the rut that dance music seems to have got itself into.'

She was also very aware of the delicate position she found herself in with the band. They really had to outdo themselves on the second LP, without overproducing it. In discussing the question of media attention *vs* respect from record-buyers Sade was quick to admit, 'I don't actually think we have that respect from the public. It's as fickle as the speed at which something becomes so big. You can lose it as quickly as you make it. The only way you maintain that is by putting a lot of care into something. We might establish ourselves better after this next album.'

The second half of 1985 had to be spent crafting the second album and preparing for the first American tour. All interviews and photo sessions were put on hold.

'There's a problem of time with me,' said Sade. 'That's because I'm also involved with writing the songs. And I don't just walk into the studio, sing my part, then walk out. I'm not being arrogant about it – that's just a fact. I'm very involved so I don't have a lot of free time.'

By the time the group had six new songs 'in the can', Sade was breathing a bit more easily. 'We're pretty happy with what we've done so far, and that's all we can ask at this moment,' she admitted amidst the production of the *Promise* album. 'We've been able to indulge in a few luxuries on this album . . . like, for instance, we've used *real* strings on some of the tracks as opposed to the synth string box we used on *Diamond Life*, but essentially it hasn't differed too much from our first album recording. Robin Millar is the credited producer, although Stuart and myself were heavily involved at all stages and we have written all the tracks, so things are pretty much the same.

'The thing I most enjoy now is one day passing without some major trauma – because we've had a lot of setbacks this year, personal things that have been quite destructive. So if one day goes by without a crisis, that's what I like doing.'

Unfortunately, during the final stages of the recording process, in October of 1985, Sade's father died suddenly.

Recalling her mother's relationship with her father, Sade had once commented, 'I'm sure my mother was still madly in love with my father, but he was terribly unstable. He's very bright but a very difficult person to live with. Everybody has to do everything precisely as he wants, even the way you put a cup on the table. Just rules, rules, rules! If you do something wrong, he gets hysterical.'

At the time of his death, her father held the post of a university professor in Nigeria. Although her career was soaring at the time of her last visit to see her father, Mr Adu was quite unimpressed with the fact that his daughter had become a pop star. Sade recalls that final visit: 'We were driving along listening to a Kool & the Gang song on the radio, and he said to me, "This is a great song. I hope one day that you make a record that's a worldwide success like this." And I said, "Dad, we're no. 1 in Germany." But he wouldn't listen.'

As mentioned earlier, a letter that her father had written to her with the phrase 'promise of hope' in it prompted the title of the group's second album. It was to exceed all the expectations riding on it.

The torchy jazz number 'Is It a Crime?' opens the *Promise* album and is the outstanding cut on the LP. The song is a desperate plea from a passionate former lover, and the band is in excellent form. Sweeping and dramatic in intensity, the piece is both smooth and raw in texture and is filled with thrilling crescendos, Sade's self-penned lyrics taking her vocally from a whisper to an emotional wail. With its breaks and peaks, 'Is It a Crime?' shows off perfectly – vocally as well as instrumentally – how well the four members of the group work together as a unit.

'Sweetest Taboo', which was written by Sade Adu and percussionist Martin Ditcham, is a peppy pop samba complete with the sound of rain beating on the windowsill – and enough acoustic space for Adu to display multi-tracked vocal dynamics. She sounds much more confident on every cut of this album, but 'Sweetest Taboo' captures her in a much warmer and more relaxed mood than is evident on *Diamond Life*, with its more distant vocal style.

In 'War of the Hearts', Sade's lyrics are so unobtrusively interwoven into Stuart's music that her voice is utilized in the mix as though it were one of the instruments. As she calls for a truce in domestic battling, the boys in the band weave an intoxicating musical spell around her, strongly suggestive of a Caribbean calypso beat, punctuated by Matthewman's exquisite sax.

According to Sade, ' "Jezebel" is about the sort of girl other girls don't like, somebody who is on the outside, and nobody really understands.' The plaintive ode finds Adu in her story-telling role, recounting the tale of a girl who feels that she does not fit into any preconceived category.

The light, medium-paced ballad 'Mr Wrong' finds Sade giving advice to the lovelorn, while 'Never as Good as the First Time' is a zesty jam for the band, with Ms Adu delivering words of wisdom to a bossa nova be-

'Fear' is a clever but touching little melodrama about a matador's lady waiting for her matador to return from the bull-ring. Is he going to come home triumphant – or is he going to come home in a box? On this Adu/Matthewman composition, Sade – who admits to a passion for Spain – sings half the words in Spanish. Enhancing the audio travelogue is a brilliant Spanish guitar solo by Carlos Bannell. *Olé!*

'Tar Baby' and 'Maureen' are the two most introspective numbers on the album, reflecting the personal life of Sade Adu. 'Tar Baby' is a song about a white woman giving birth to a brown baby. The obviously autobiographical lyric describes the first time the white grandmother lays eyes on the baby, and how prejudices can be melted with love.

'Maureen' is a loving lament for a deceased friend, but is anything but maudlin. Although sad, its message seems to be: 'I'm sorry that you're not here to meet my new friends, but I'll carry on for you in my thoughts.' For anyone who has lost a close friend, the song is a heart-touching remembrance that is warm and bitter-sweet rather than painful.

Again, for some unknown reason, on the cassette and compact disc versions of the *Promise* album the record company has added two extra cuts: a ballad called 'You're Not the Man' and an instrumental jam written by Andrew Hale entitled 'Punch Drunk'. In America 'You're Not the Man' is the flip side to the single version of 'Sweetest Taboo'. There are two British pressings of the singles 'Sweetest Taboo' and 'Is It a Crime?'. 'Sweetest Taboo' is on one side of the American 'import' 12-inch single, an 'extended version' including an additional minute of music; another elongated number, 'You're Not the Man' appears on the flip side. The 12-inch British pressing of the song 'Is It a Crime?' not only features the cut 'Punch Drunk' on the back of it, but has the instrumental 'Wired' following the hit on the 'A' side. Another 'collector's item' from Sade is a high-spirited song entitled 'Spirit', which is available only on the 'B' side of the 'Smooth Operator' 7-inch single (both British and American versions).

The production of the *Promise* album and the sheer quality of its music demonstrate how much the band has developed since its first album. Sade's lyric-writing is consistently entertaining and displays great insight, while the band's compositions show off their craft to new advantage. *Promise* is not necessarily a better album than *Diamond Life*, more a progression from it that further underlines the band's identity and Sade Adu's arresting vocal prowess. Although there is no doubt that she is an integral part of the Sade ensemble, she is obviously destined to be a star in her own right — even though the team of Adu/Matthewman/Denman/Hale may continue as a creative unit for the next 30 years.

The *Promise* album became an instant international smash. Released in November 1985, it was no. 1 in Italy and the Netherlands by January of 1986, in the Top Ten in West Germany, Britain, France and the USA, and in the Top Twenty in Australia, Japan and Canada. In the United States, during the week of 15 February 1986, *Promise* knocked Barbra Streisand's *Broadway Album* off the no. 1 spot on the *Billboard* chart, having sold over a million copies in its first seven weeks of release there. The single 'Sweetest Taboo' went on to become a no. 1 hit as well.

Reviewing her recordings, *Rolling Stone* observed: 'Although her dusky alto croon is alluringly sensual, Sade is ultimately about control.' *People* magazine called the *Promise* album 'cool, diffident and a tinge sardonic . . . a delicious combination. Her singing has elegance.' The review went on to echo the feelings of many a critic/fan of Sade's: 'Matthewman's saxophone behind Sade's vocal on "War of the Hearts" displays some of the sensuality of the Lester Young/Billie Holiday records.'

Comparisons between the singing, style, phrasing and emotiveness of Sade Adu and Billie Holiday have been constant since the début of *Diamond Life*. Though they in no way suggest any lack of individuality on the part of Sade, it is reasonable to claim that no female singer since Holiday has captured the blues so exquisitely on vinyl.

As for parallels between Holiday and herself as women, though she freely admits that Holiday is her idol, Sade has distinct views on the subject: 'I believe she suffered, but I know Billie Holiday too well to ever compare myself to her. Some of it is fantasy. I've lived. I've had an unusual sort of background, but I don't

71

think you necessarily have to have a lot of pain to appreciate what other people feel and to communicate that emotion. Pain, you know, is relative to each person's experience anyway. If we never sold a record in America, and our stuff helped people to be aware of other singers like that, that would be good – that would be doing something. I don't think I have anything to do with Billie Holiday – or Dinah Washington – except for the fact that I've always listened to these singers. And, obviously, I guess, in some way they've influenced me. There have been parallels drawn between me and Holiday . . . and I think they are absolutely ludicrous. Probably it's men who start it, and it's because I'm female, I'm brown, I wear my hair pulled back and she wore hers the same. I think those can be the only reasons that the comparisons have come about.' Yet this is not the whole story: these two singers do seem to feel the intensity of their songs in a similar fashion and to convey it in a similar way.

Sade admits that her reason for resenting the comparison is because it could be seen to detract from her talent. 'It would bother anyone, because everybody likes to think they're an original, even if they're not. Most people don't like comparisons. The one comparison I did really like was with Smokey Robinson. I didn't mind that one bit, because Smokey's a man, and I think it's quite nice to be compared to a man, because they were talking about phrasing and the way I approach a song. It's got nothing to do with sex and I appreciated that more than any other comparison.'

With regard to the frequent comment that her music invokes visions of the smoke-filled clubs of thirty years ago, Sade's response is: 'I don't really like the idea of this smoky cocktail-lounge business. It's sort of retro, nostalgic, and I like things that are timeless. I don't like to associate with any particular era. I suppose it's because what we do isn't necessarily like what's being accepted as the norm at the moment. It's just different. We don't leap up and down or spin on our heads!'

A video version of 'Sweetest Taboo' helped sell the single, and in America M-TV and the other music video stations jumped on the opportunity to air it. Shot in Spain, it was directed by B. Ward, who worked on the 'Hang on to Your Love' video. In it Sade gets to ride on horseback, perform with the band in what looks like a holiday rehearsal session, and to sing plaintively while the rain drizzles down against a picture window. The 'Is

It a Crime?' video takes place at night in a penthouse apartment from which city lights can be seen. Both videos are directed with a restraint that complements the style of the band in performance.

On Tuesday 10 December, the *Promise* tour kicked off in the middle of New York City, at the world-famous Radio City Music Hall. The gilt-ceilinged art deco entertainment palace was the ideal setting for the first American Sade concert – which was an immediate sell-out.

Opening with its classic rendition of 'Why Can't We Live Together?' the band sounded exquisite that night and the cheering crowd responded enthusiastically to the sight of the divine Miss Adu and her band. Every date of this short tour sold out immediately (the Radio City tickets in less than one hour) and Sade drew rave reviews from the east coast – 'lushly distinctive . . . winning!' (*Rolling Stone*) – to the west ('the sleekest act to arrive this year . . . exotic!': *Hollywood Reporter*). Although the tour lasted only ten days, it served to whet the American appetite for the girl with the high forehead, the plait and the haunting vocal style. It was the perfect preview for the major world tour that was to follow in 1986.

Sade, Stuart, Paul and Andrew, the established 'Sade band', arrived in the States with six additional musicians for their stage act: Martin Ditcham on percussion, Dave Early on drums, Stuart's younger brother Gordon Matthewman on trumpet, Gordon Hunter on guitar, Leroy Osbourne on backing vocals, and Jake Jacas on trombone and backing vocals.

Sade said at the time, 'The nice thing about the stage I'm at is that everything is still such a thrill. I still haven't got over that feeling before a show when you realize: "My God, they've come to see *me*. What if I can't do it?" ' Her performances showed America that she *can* do it, to perfection.

Stuart commented: 'Sade's never really relaxed on stage, which I think is part of her charm – she's quite a naive performer. With her it's not a big Vegas-type thing. Cynics think she's being cool and aloof, but she's just nervous. She's a very, very hard worker. It's tiring just being with her. Whenever we go away anywhere, we always end up staying up till 5 a.m.!'

Of the band's stage show, Robert Elms has revealed: 'Afterwards it'll usually be her producer Robin Millar who she'll ask what she was like, because he knows her strength and limitations. An "all right" from him is better than a "brilliant" from anyone else.'

Sade's personal assistant Rhonda Paster goes on tour with the band to make sure that everything happens on schedule. 'The last tour, for instance,' she explains, 'was like having eight children. Apart from checking on the promoters, I had to make sure that everything was right when we arrived for the show. Then I had to get everyone up and out of the hotel in the mornings. The person who's physically most difficult to get up in the mornings is Stuart. But the one who is *always* late is Sade. What I had to do was tell the band to be down by 9.15 and tell Sade nine o'clock.'

In 1985 the group's *Diamond Life* album received an accolade from Britain's record industry: the 'Best Album' prize in the BPI Awards. In 1986, in America, when the annual Grammy Awards were handed out by the US music industry, Sade was nominated 'Best New Artist' along with Julian Lennon, A-Ha, Katrina & the Waves and Freddie Jackson. Sade took the prize as 'Best New Artist' on 25 February when the winners were announced, much to the excitement of her millions of fans across America.

Despite all the acclaim, the excitement and the column inches in the press, Sade Adu remains her own strongest critic. 'I'll never be 100-per-cent satisfied with anything I do,' she admits, 'which actually seems a miserable and depressing prospect, but it's just the way I am. I do get enjoyment out of what I'm doing, but I think I'll always feel there's somewhere further and stronger I can go.'

It's good to know that while she's sitting on top of the world, trying to get used to success, this is just the beginning for Sade.

S A D E
I N   F A S H I O N

One of the reasons for Sade Adu's incredible international success is the fact that she is alarmingly beautiful and chic in a way that is entirely individual to her. Her background in the fashion design industry has obviously made her highly aware of the importance of self-presentation.

OF HER APPEARANCE, she has said, self-deprecatingly – and laughing: 'I don't think I'm classically good-looking. In fact, I think I'm a bit strange-looking. I mean, my forehead sits on top of my head like a large grapefruit!'

Yet *Vogue* magazine, Bible of the international fashion scene, has christened Sade one of 'the most beautiful black women today'. Her use of make-up has certainly attained the *Vogue* seal of approval: 'On Sade, brilliant red lips – the first thing you notice on her album cover *Promise* . . . classic red lips – very appealing against brown skin.'

The *New York Daily News* recently observed that 'The British rock star has made ponytails and pigtails the hairstyle of the moment. . . [and] her backless dresses are being copied by dress manufacturers from London to LA!'

Karl Lagerfeld, renowned fashion designer to the rich and famous, is an enthusiastic Sade devotee. Both her appearance and her sound intrigue him. Lagerfeld, the former Coco Chanel protégé, raves about the 'Smooth Operator'.

Lagerfeld has decreed, from his offices in Paris, 'Fashion is change. To be into it you have to be a kind of intellectual opportunist.' He has further noted that 'Music is the most important fashion influence, if you ask me – more important than movies or anything. It's like fashion; it has to be the latest of the latest.'

In 1985, the girls who worked in Lagerfeld's studio emulated the looks of Madonna. Now they all dress like Sade. Karl also proclaims that he is influenced by the fashion sense of Ms Adu as well, and her picture now graces the wall of his office for understated inspiration.'

What are Sade's make-up tips? 'False eyelashes, definitely. They just project everything. Though the secret is only to wear about four, on each outer eye corner.' She keeps her cosmetic essentials to a minimum: 'For me, a brow pencil and lipstick for definition, from either Yves St Laurent, Cosmetics à la Carte or Molton Brown.' For photographic sessions Sade likes to rely upon the direction of a good professional make-up artist, 'because', she says, 'it's one less thing to worry about.

'I've worn hoop earrings for the last ten years,' says Sade of her jewellery. 'Now everybody is wearing them. She claims that she likes only 'simple, basic things', and explains, paradoxically, 'I've never liked fashion, but I've always liked clothes. I'm not a fashion victim, I'm not obsessed. I like quirky one-offs that people wouldn't necessarily buy. I like people who are one-offs, too; people who appear to be a stereotype and then go totally against the grain.'

According to her, 'I won't buy clothes because I've seen them in a magazine. I do buy designer clothes, though. I know it's very trendy to like Jean-Paul Gaultier, but I really *do* like his stuff. Some of his clothes make me sick and I wouldn't have them in my wardrobe, never mind on my back, but he's got a sense of humour and he's quirky.'

Sade confesses that she spends 'a ridiculous amount of money on clothes,' and in particular has spent 'a ridiculous amount of money on a Jean-Paul. But that isn't *why* I buy it. I can't stand people who buy Yamamoto because it's Yamamoto, just to feel safe. I buy things because they are right, not because I can turn them inside out and throw them over a chair with the label showing.'

She also claims that she purchases some 'incredibly cheap things' because it's fun 'mixing cheap with

expensive'. She also prefers pants to dresses, 'because I can move a lot better in them'.

As far as her hair is concerned, she prefers it 'off my face – because of the height of my forehead, not many styles suit me.' (However, she appears in *Absolute Beginners* with a very attractive short crop with a spiky fringe framing her expressive face.)

Being overweight is *never* a problem: 'On the contrary, I have to make sure I don't go underweight.'

Her friend Rhonda Paster confirms this: 'Sade does love her food. She doesn't love sweets so much as savoury things. She can eat like an absolute pig and never put on a pound. You've never seen such excitement as when she spots a hot-dog stand. She *loves* hot dogs!' It seems that we need not bother to look forward to a book entitled *The Sade Diet*.

As for the colours she wears, according to Sade the choice depends upon what she sees in the mirror in the morning. 'If I look healthy and brown,' she explains, 'I wear something vibrant. If I'm washed out I'll wear black. I haven't got a formula for the way I dress. My memory's so short, if I had, I'd lose it!

'I don't feel comfortable in overtly sexy clothes,' says Sade. 'People often say to me I look great in a tight top and something where you can see my bum . . . If it looks sexy by coincidence, fine. But I don't like that contrived sexy look; it's too self-conscious. There's nothing wrong with sexy, I don't mean that. But if it's contrived it looks uncomfortable. It overtakes your whole person, the way you behave and everything – you flirt more, for sure.

'Madonna?' ponders Sade of the 'Material Girl' and her wardrobe. 'I wouldn't be seen dead in most of what she wears, but I do like the way she looks. She gets a lot of flak, but she's got a positive direction. There's no doubt that she does play directly on sex, but quite frankly I think she's enjoyable.'

Since Sade, until not so long ago, was studying to become a fashion designer, does she fancy the idea of designing her own clothes? Unfortunately not, it seems. 'I don't get any time to do any of my own designing,' she explains, 'but I have friends who make stuff that I've partly designed. I also get things that they've designed entirely. But at the same time I get designer labels too.' Again, she stresses that she's not a 'fashion victim': 'I'm not obsessed by labels. I get hysterical when people start talking about second-hand clothes like they were designed by "Srift Schopper", a famous German designer. Or "Second Handy Schopper" – he's very popular too! I don't just buy designer labels for the sake of it. So I've got a real mixture of clothes that range from the extremely, ludicrously overpriced to the ludicrously underpriced.

'I like timeless things,' she says of the things she owns. 'My proudest possessions are my Profil flat-screen TV and my car, a 1958 Wolseley, even though I don't have any time to drive it any more. The most outrageous thing I've got since I became successful is a house with a heated towel-rail! I've always dreamed of that. And I've always loved Bill Withers, Marvin Gaye, Nina Simone and Billie Holiday. I like things that aren't necessarily associated with an era. Just quality things that you look at and say, "Oh, that's lovely," not "Oh, that's 'forties or 'fifties" or "That's the 'eighties," – you know what I mean? Things that look timeless – just things that are classic and will last forever. I'm an old-fashioned girl. I think anything good lasts.'

Like the *Diamond Life* album, for instance?

In one sense, certainly, Sade considers that the music is timeless: 'I think if I had started making music ten years ago, or ten years ahead . . . I would have a similar approach. There would be songs with stories; we would play with feeling between each other. I think it would be very much as it is . . . it isn't really a reaction, because I've never really been part of that. I've never really got involved with the current scene. It's not my thing, so it makes no difference what period we started, really. It's a coincidence.

'A lot of songs are a part of me,' she says of her song-writing. 'Some are fantasies of course, but I don't want to be self-indulgent when I write songs. I just want to put some feeling across that not only me but other people can enjoy.

'I like jazz,' she admits, 'but only recently, say in the last five years, have I been able to listen to anything that doesn't have a vocal in it. Now I can hear another instrument as a voice, so at least my taste is a bit broader. I used to only really listen to soul. That is, I like things sung soulfully, songs with a story, not just black soul . . . A good song is a good song, but a *good* song has some sort of emotion and moves you in some way . . . I call it all soul.

'I'm frightened of anyone for one minute thinking that we're trying to be a jazz band, because if we were we could do it a lot better than we're doing now. We don't sit around and say, "Right, we're going to create this sound." It happens too naturally for us to intellectualize about [it]. When we create a song, it's just . . . the way it goes. Our music is clearly pop, because it's easy to understand.'

It seems that she became a sensation instantly, but she is quick to correct this impression: 'I haven't popped out of nowhere, not as extremely as people think. We have been together for about four-and-a-half years now, so we've actually been working fairly consistently, and . . . it hasn't been that easy.'

How has success changed Sade? According to *People* magazine, in March 1986, she had personally earned $10 million. However, she feels that she is pretty much unaffected by wealth. 'It's a relief, but it's weird, because not having money never got me down, ever. If I wanted something badly I always managed to get it. I've never relied on a man to provide me with anything. I've always known it would be o.k. one day,' she says.

Planning her career around money alone is not even a possibility: 'There is absolutely nothing wrong whatsoever with progress and trying new things, but to gauge your entire existence on financial reward is incredibly restrictive in terms of creating. If we make tons and tons of money through our music, fine. I'm not going to give it back to the record company. But my main object isn't to make tons and tons of money.

'People's reactions to me [are] a bit overwhelming,' she admits. 'It's hard to walk in the streets in England now, and it's impossible to be anonymous. It bothers me, but is something that I'm going to have to get used to. Success is not overwhelming, though, because it is what you are ultimately striving for.

'The fame makes it hard to wander around Europe or England. But you have to expect these intrusions. The money hasn't changed me except for making my life a little easier. My cousin wanted to go see her Mum in Nigeria, so I bought her a ticket for Christmas, and it was no different from buying her a new pair of shoes or taking her out for a meal. Of course, now I have a warm flat instead of a freezing cold one,' she adds, laughing.

'There is a fear of developing a feeling that I don't want to lose what I've got. But most of my friends are poor, so I don't think they're gonna let me drift off too far. You must be careful not to want success for the wrong reasons. You can't allow money to be the motive for success.

'I miss simple things,' she explains, 'like going shopping and getting lost in your own thoughts as you wander along the street. It's an impossibility now, because I've got to remember that at any second somebody could come up to me. You can't consider it as an intrusion, because it's exactly what you've set yourself to be. I couldn't just go to the swimming-pool on a hot Sunday afternoon – that sort of thing I miss. [I'd like] a bit more time to myself and to be with people – that's how I relax, by being with people.'

'COOLLY ELEGANT ... SMOULDERING BEAUTY!'

– US

The media attention that she now receives makes Sade very conscious of everything that she does. 'You feel everything you say has to be precious,' she claims, 'because people are looking at you with much more open ears and eyes.

'Some facets of what we do are therapeutic. It's all the other things you have to do, the phone calls you have to make to explain you don't want something done *that* way, you want it done *that* way, otherwise it's going to go all wrong. That's what stops the whole thing from being quite relaxing and makes it a headache. But actually recording is a relaxing thing.

'I'm very busy. . . There's no lifestyle, just very chaotic [living]. I came back to my flat after making the "Taboo" video in Spain and I thought it had been ransacked. But it hadn't . . . I'd done it myself when I was packing to leave!

'I don't mind living out of a suitcase, but I don't like the practical problems it involves. There's a permanent problem with creased clothes. When you're constantly moving and constantly packing and unpacking, and you've got tons of stuff, it's a burden. You feel like a bag woman!' She laughs at the dilemma.

'I don't have time to be Sade. . . But we're all good friends in the band, which has made it easier for me, because I've had a lot of mishaps and personal problems. It's been one of those years. There's a line in "Never as Good as the First Time": "One day chicken, the next day feathers." This year was just feathers,' she reflected, looking back on 1985. 'Chicken comes next year, we hope.'

She was granted her wish: *Promise* became the international multi-million best-selling album of the year, she won the Best New Artist Grammy Award and she made her movie début in the musical film *Absolute Beginners*. It looks like she's not only achieving the metaphor in her song, but the whole hen-coop of chickens!

LIVING THE MULTI-PLATINUM LIFE

Hit songs, million-selling albums, magazine cover-stories, world tours, holidays in Sri Lanka, international awards and monetary rewards – what more could life hold in store for Sade? Becoming a movie star, maybe? Her portrayal of Athene Duncannon, the glamorous torch singer at the Chez Nobody jazz club in the film *Absolute Beginners*, is a glittering achievement in the 'diamond life' of Ms Adu.

BASED ON THE memorable novel by Colin MacInnes, the musical *Absolute Beginners* captures the brashness, bravado, energy and excitement of London in the late 'fifties . . . a world of jazz clubs, coffee bars, a sleazy, criminal subculture, gangs of teddy boys and teenagers out to discover what life is all about. A city on the verge of the youth revolution, London was described by MacInnes at the time as being 'as ripe for conquest as Balzac's Paris'.

Drug dealers, jazz musicians, young people whiling away the hours over steaming cups of espresso in Soho dives, blacks and whites elbow to elbow in an uneasy co-existence. This is the 1958 time-capsule that MacInnes created in his celebrated trilogy of novels *Absolute Beginners, City of Spades* and *Mr Love and Mr Justice*. The elaborately filmed version of *Absolute Beginners* is the embodiment of the dream of filmmaker Julien Temple, who set out to show on celluloid 'the whole change of Britain in the 'fifties – everything from the racial tensions to the impact of rock 'n' roll, the fashions, the frozen food and the craze for cars with fins'. Although he was only a child at the time, he remembers 'those long sunsets down Oxford Street, when you'd see a girl with nothing on but a polka-dot mac walking into the "100" club. People seem to think that things all started with the Beatles and the Stones. In fact the late 'fifties was a colourful time.'

With a cast that includes, besides Sade and stars Patsy Kensit and Eddie O'Connell, James Fox, David Bowie, Ray Davies of the Kinks, Ronald Fraser, Lionel Blair, Alan Freeman, Eric Sykes and Sylvia Syms, amid a host of newcomers, *Absolute Beginners* marks Temple's transition from director of short music videos to feature-filmmaker.

Temple is especially noted for his work on Bowie's 'Jazzin' for Blue Jean', the Rolling Stones' 'Undercover', and Sade's video versions of 'Smooth Operator' and 'Your Love Is King'. It was always his intention to make *Absolute Beginners* a cinema event on a grand scale. 'A lot of movies lately have just plastered on a hit single from a known band because it's good for business. We've gone back to the old style, where the songs are an integral part of the story. They forward the action, they forward the characterization. You can't make a film with Sade and David Bowie and expect it to be an art-house film.'

In the film, Sade Adu is seen on stage at the Chez Nobody club in a glittering strapless cocktail dress singing her self-penned song 'Killer Blow'. Petite and gamine, with her hair short and close to the head, like an elf's cap, she commands attention both visually and aurally. The sequence comes just before the film's grand climax, a *West Side Story*-like version of the Notting Hill race riots, complete with knife fights and frenetic ensemble choreography. The whole look of the film is distinctively fantasy-like. Colours are never muted but constantly accentuated – producing a vibrant video dream. Sade herself is in a sapphire blue gown and has ruby red lips.

Although the critical response to the film as a whole was mixed, the press was unanimously in approval of the visual aesthetics, music and dancing. Sade's role may only have been a guest spot, but her fleeting appearance was one of the film's highlights and many reviewers would have liked to see a greater contribution from her.

Audiences were certainly left thirsting for more.

Reviewers wrote: 'An "Absolute" treat for the eyes
. . . Sade is photographed like something out of an
elaborate hophead dream . . . It'll be playing midnight
shows for a century!' (Mike Clark in *USA Today*);
'*Absolute Beginners* is spectacular . . . one of the most
ambitious and exciting movies of the decade . . . This
movie is sheer pleasure . . . there's always something
fantastic to look at and wonderful to hear' (John
Powers, *L.A. Weekly*); '*Absolute Beginners* is
absolutely breathtaking . . . If there are elements of
MTV here, and harbingers of film and fashion trends to
come, there's Balanchine too. And David Bowie in a
swell tap dance. And Sade just plain singing. It's class
stuff, enhanced by brilliant primary colours. And you
can't take your eyes off it for a minute' (David Hinckley,
The New York Daily News); 'Sade, Ray Davies and the
snakily elegant David Bowie appear in elaborate
production numbers – upmarket rock videos, really –
and Julien Temple, a master director of the short music
form, revs up the visuals so that everything looks like a
display in the biggest, fanciest boutique window'
(Richard Corliss, *Time*).

All in all, it looks as though the film will open up
many more opportunities for Sade in films.

The possibilities are now endless for the lady who
'always knew it would be o.k.'. As she admits: 'I've
been lucky. I could run around the world being a star
now if I let a producer make the records and I just did
the singing track. But I write the songs with Stuart and
we are there for the whole process. I often go to bed at
6 a.m. Anyone who works in the City would have a
heart attack after a fortnight if they worked in music. I'll
have to have a break in a year or so and go to
Clacton-on-Sea to convalesce and be wheeled about
by nuns!' she says, laughing.

Instant success does not mean endless days of wine
and roses. In fact when things get moving too fast, it
can all turn into a nightmare. In March of 1986, Sade's
'diamond life' was getting to be a bit too much for her,
and she cut short her spring concert tour of Europe
quite abruptly.

Since parting company with Robert Elms, Sade had
been dating nightclub impresario Spike Denton.
Several British newspapers got hold of the news that
Denton had dropped Sade to return to his former
girlfriend and made a big deal of it. Suddenly Sade
was all over the front pages of the popular press. On

Tuesday, 18 March, Sade and her band were performing in Frankfurt, Germany. The show began 55 minutes after the scheduled curtain time, and Sade made her entrance on stage, sang four songs, then suddenly broke into tears amid the fifth selection. 'I hope you hang on to your love, because I can't hang on to mine,' she sobbed to the audience. At that, she walked off stage and cut the show short.

'I was shattered, exhausted – not physically but mentally,' Sade explained later. 'I was drained, by all the lies that have been said and written about me and my love for Spike . . . When people snipe at me and tell loads of lies, it hurts so much . . . I'm asking to be given a fair break. Is that too much to ask?

'When I was in Frankfurt, I'd had a bellyful – and that doesn't mean I was pregnant,' she said – able to joke about it now that it was just a memory. 'I was tired, and not just with touring. I could cope with touring for the rest of my life if that were all we were doing, if we weren't having pictures taken or making videos or doing interviews. That's o.k. But any sort of emotional interference tires you out more than straightforward physical strain.'

After the incident, Sade pulled herself together and resumed the tour. According to her, 'If it hadn't been for the fact that I'm responsible to the band, that they are my friends and we are very important to each other, I would have given up, gone into brief hiding. I would have become like Howard Hughes and started covering the furniture in polythene. To have complete sanity and order in my life I would have become completely insane.'

Three days after the Frankfurt 'walkout', Sade and her band were scheduled to perform six concert dates at the Théâtre de l'Olympia in Paris. The first three shows went quite well, and included the addition of the group's version of William de Vaughn's song 'Be Thankful For What You've Got'. When Sade Adu returned to the stage for an encore, the crowd cheeringly chanted, 'Diva! Diva!'

On the following Monday, after completing three of the six scheduled shows, the band received tragic news. Ethna Matthewman, mother of Stuart and Gordon, had become seriously ill. The tour was cut short, and Mrs Matthewman died later that week. The rest of the Paris dates and additional appearances scheduled for Italy were all postponed indefinitely. The band was grief-stricken.

News of the two incidents, first Frankfurt, then Paris, spread like wildfire in music circles. Would the tour continue? Would Sade be able to carry on in spite of the pressure that the press was putting on her?

When all the gossip and rumours subsided, Sade and her band were able to put the situation in perspective and move on to other things. The cancelled tour dates had been setbacks, but they were hardly the end of the world. Sade is now able to dismiss the Frankfurt situation as a one-time emotional *impasse*.

The pace of life and the money-motivation of the music business impose their own pressures. Looking back on her recording career, she remembers what it was like at the beginning – not so very long ago: 'It wasn't difficult to get a deal. It was difficult to get a *decent* deal. You only get that when you've sold millions of albums and are re-negotiating.' From that moment on, she has of course been marketed, sometimes in ways that were not to her liking: 'I think the music business is no worse than any other business involved in selling a product. The only reason we are aware of it is because they are selling personalities. And a toothpaste doesn't turn around and say, "I don't like the way I looked in that last commercial!" There are a lot of people in the biz I respect, but I wonder how some people got there, what they are doing there and when they are going to leave.'

Has her striking beauty helped her to achieve fame more quickly? Sade confesses that it has never been a hindrance: 'It's just like the way you would sell yourself in any situation. Like if you're in a club and you want to go home with a particular person: if that's your motive, then you use certain things to sell yourself. That's the way people are. Then again: you have certain things that sell you without your even trying. That's what you're given, that's what you have, that's what you live with. So of course it might help to get people interested in the first place. But unless there's something to be interested *in*, the interest won't last anyway. I'm really open to more criticism and suspicion as I am than if I looked like a monster. Then I'd be all right: you know, "the talented monster", not "just another pretty face", as they say. So, if anything, it works against me in terms of being taken . . . uh, listened to. I was going to say "taken seriously", but why should anyone take us [the band] *that* seriously?'

Sade does not like to be labelled, especially not for her colour. 'I consider myself me,' she declares. 'My dad's black and my mum's white, and I just don't look at life like that. I was brought up not to even question the colour of people's skins. We were brought up to question what's *underneath* it.'

The same views are reflected in her outlook on the American music industry. 'I don't like segregation,' she affirms. 'Music is something which should be available to all people. When you go into a club there is no colour bar on the dance floor, so why should it apply to radio stations? Unfortunately, it does. It doesn't only apply to black and white, it also applies to heavy metal, pop, all that. It's such a big place with such big corporations everywhere that in order to feel safe they have to categorize things. I've always listened to black music because I like the sound of the black voice, so it wouldn't be bad to be successful in the same place I have always loved. But I usually figure if something is good enough, people find it anyway, and you're gonna get the exposure and ultimately spread. The only reason people picked up on us in the first place was because we had an audience.'

She continues: 'Most things around are very similar in every respect, the music and the way people look. In order to be in a band, you have to have certain colours in your hair – still! Our image is striking because it is different, not because it is particularly outstanding. The public has not got such bad taste after all, if you know what I mean. There are quite a lot of fairly intelligent people around who, if allowed to make their own decisions, will.'

Her determination and her attitude to life have greatly benefited her. 'Of course I've struggled in every way. I've never had anything come easily to me other than the creative side. [But] I've never been taught to be scared of someone because of their authority or position. That's partly because of my mother's attitude.' (As described earlier, Anne Adu displayed great courage in leaving Sade's father in Nigeria and heading back to England with her two small children: 'My mother left with no clothes, no furniture, no money . . . nothing! She literally had to start again,' Sade recalls. Her own attitude to others is equally uncompromising.) 'I think I'm no more likely to be scared of, say, the managing director of CBS than I am to be scared of the man in the corner shop who's aggressive when you buy your papers. It's to do with the person, not the position. That's helped me a lot because I don't allow the mystique to affect my judgement of a situation because of fear. I don't have that kind of fear. My feelings don't change because someone maybe has the power to destroy [me]. Because the more you compromise, the more you're defeated by them, the less respect these people have for you, and the less power you have in a situation. So basically it's best just to be honest and not to worry too much about the consequences.

'Our society is a sexist one,' Sade observes. 'That's more obvious in the music business than in the world in general. It affects me as a person – not necessarily so much as an artist. It is annoying if people think you're dozy and don't give you a chance, but then they're usually pretty dozy anyway and not worth the time of day.'

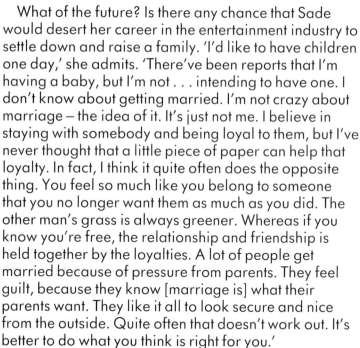

What of the future? Is there any chance that Sade would desert her career in the entertainment industry to settle down and raise a family. 'I'd like to have children one day,' she admits. 'There've been reports that I'm having a baby, but I'm not . . . intending to have one. I don't know about getting married. I'm not crazy about marriage – the idea of it. It's just not me. I believe in staying with somebody and being loyal to them, but I've never thought that a little piece of paper can help that loyalty. In fact, I think it quite often does the opposite thing. You feel so much like you belong to someone that you no longer want them as much as you did. The other man's grass is always greener. Whereas if you know you're free, the relationship and friendship is held together by the loyalties. A lot of people get married because of pressure from parents. They feel guilt, because they know [marriage is] what their parents want. They like it all to look secure and nice from the outside. Quite often that doesn't work out. It's better to do what you think is right for you.'

At the moment, Sade Adu is too busy with Stuart, Andrew and Paul making music and videos and touring the globe to consider marrying. Indeed, finding time for any activity not related to her career is virtually impossible. However, she has claimed: 'I don't feel the need to have hobbies.' Nor, despite that voice redolent of late nights and smoke-filled dives, is she the nightclub type: 'I don't like nightclubs that much. I was never somebody who spent my life down at the Blitz. That's too boring. I'd rather go to the pictures or out for a meal with friends.' She especially likes Robert Mitchum movies.

Living life on her own terms means, of course, singing what she wants to sing, for her own reasons: 'I used to perform "Cry Me a River" on stage, but that was because it's a great song, not because Julie London sang it,' she has said. She likes what she likes and is not swayed by the public's opinion of what she should be doing. She prefers old friends like her 1958 Wolseley automobile in preference to the shiny new Rolls-Royce which she could now afford and has even said, 'I wouldn't drive a Roller if someone gave me one!' She is her own girl, living the 'diamond life' by her own definition, not someone else's.

Movie star . . . chanteuse . . . beautiful, . . . cover girl original, classy . . . Sade is sitting on top of the world. She's the toast of six continents, and fortunately for all of us who have been touched by her entrancing music, this is just the beginning.

D I S C O G R A P H Y
ALBUMS

(1) Diamond Life
Release date: July 1984 (February 1985 in USA and Canada)

Side one:
1. 'Smooth Operator'
Words and music by Sade Adu and Ray St John
Time: 4 minutes, 54 seconds
Producer: Robin Millar
2. 'Your Love Is King'
Words by Sade Adu; music by Sade Adu and Stuart Matthewman
Time: 3 minutes, 57 seconds
Producer: Robin Millar
3. 'Hang on to Your Love'
Words by Sade Adu; music by Sade Adu and Stuart Matthewman
Time: 5 minutes, 58 seconds
Producer: Robin Millar
4. 'Frankie's First Affair'
Words by Sade Adu; music by Sade Adu and Stuart Matthewman
Time: 4 minutes, 33 seconds
Producer: Robin Millar
5. 'When Am I Going to Make a Living?'
Words by Sade Adu; music by Sade Adu and Stuart Matthewman
Time: 3 minutes, 25 seconds
Producer: Robin Millar

Side two:
1. 'Cherry Pie'
Words by Sade Adu; music by Sade Adu, Stuart Matthewman, Andrew Hale and Paul S. Denman
Time: 6 minutes, 16 seconds
Producer: Robin Millar
2. 'Sally'
Words by Sade Adu; music by Sade Adu and Stuart Matthewman
Time: 5 minutes, 19 seconds
Producer: Robin Millar
3. 'I Will Be Your Friend'
Words by Sade Adu; music by Sade Adu and Stuart Matthewman
Time: 4 minutes, 39 seconds
Producer: Robin Millar
4. 'Why Can't We Live Together?'
Words and music by Timmy Thomas
Time: 5 minutes, 27 seconds
Producer: Robin Millar

Album personnel:
Sade:
   Sade Adu, vocals
   Stuart Matthewman, saxophone and guitar
   Andrew Hale, keyboards
   Paul S. Denman, bass guitar

Additional musicians:
   Dave Early, drums and percussion
   Martin Ditcham, percussion
   Paul Cooke, drums
   Terry Bailey, trumpet
   Gordon Matthewman, trumpet

Technical staff:
   Mike Pela, production engineer
   Ben Rogan, engineer on 'Why Can't We Live Together?'

Recorded at the Power Plant, London

(2) Promise

Release date: November 1985

Side one:

1. 'Is It a Crime?'
Words by Sade Adu; music by Sade
Adu, Stuart Matthewman and
Andrew Hale
Time: 6 minutes, 18 seconds
Producer: Robin Millar
2. 'The Sweetest Taboo'
Words by Sade Adu; music by Sade
Adu and Martin Ditcham
Time: 4 minutes, 31 seconds
Producer: Robin Millar
3. 'War of the Hearts'
Words by Sade Adu; music by Sade
Adu and Stuart Matthewman
Time: 6 minutes, 46 seconds
Producer: Robin Millar
4. 'Jezebel'
Words by Sade Adu; music by Sade
Adu and Stuart Matthewman
Time: 5 minutes, 27 seconds
Producer: Robin Millar

Side two:

1. 'Mr Wrong'
Words by Sade Adu; music by Sade
Adu, Stuart Matthewman, Paul S.
Denman and Andrew Hale
Time: 2 minutes, 46 seconds
Producer: Robin Millar
2. 'Never as Good as the First Time'
Words by Sade Adu; music by Sade
Adu and Stuart Matthewman
Time: 4 minutes, 57 seconds
Producers: Robin Millar, Ben
Rogan, Mike Pela, Sade Adu, Stuart
Matthewman, Andrew Hale and
Paul S. Denman
3. 'Fear'
Words by Sade Adu; music by Sade
Adu and Stuart Matthewman
Time: 4 minutes, 6 seconds
Producer: Robin Millar
4. 'Tar Baby'
Words by Sade Adu; music by Sade

Adu and Stuart Matthewman
Time: 3 minutes, 55 seconds
Producer: Robin Millar
5. 'Maureen'
Words by Sade Adu; music by Sade
Adu, Andrew Hale and Paul S.
Denman
Time: 4 minutes, 18 seconds
Producers: Ben Rogan, Sade Adu,
Stuart Matthewman, Andrew Hale
and Paul S. Denman, mixed by Mike
Pela

Album personnel:

Sade:
    Sade Adu, vocals
    Stuart Matthewman, saxophone
    and guitar
    Paul S. Denman, bass guitar
    Andrew Hale, keyboards

Additional musicians:
    Dave Early, drums and percussion
    Martin Ditcham, percussion
    Terry Bailey, trumpet
    Pete Beachill, trombone
    Jake Jacas, background vocals
    Carlos Bonnell, guitar on 'Fear'

Technical staff:
    Mike Pela, production engineer
    Nick Ingham, string arranger

Recorded at the Power Plant,
London and Studio Miraval, France

(3) Absolute Beginners

(original soundtrack)
Release date: March 1986
Produced by Clive Langer and Alan
Winstanley
Side one:
1. 'Absolute Beginners' performed by
David Bowie
Words and music by David Bowie
Time: 8 minutes
Additional producer: David Bowie
2. 'Killer Blow' performed by Sade
Words and music by Adu, Booth

and Stabbins
Time: 4 minutes, 35 seconds
Additional producer: Robin Millar
3. 'Have You Ever Had It Blue?'
performed by Style Council
Words and music by Paul Weller
Time: 5 minutes, 36 seconds
4. 'Quiet Life' performed by Ray
Davies
Words and music by Ray Davies
Time: 2 minutes, 55 seconds
5. 'Va Va Voom' performed by Gil
Evans
Words and music by Gil Evans
Time: 3 minutes, 27 seconds

Side two:
1. 'That's Motivation' performed by
David Bowie
Words and music by David Bowie
Time: 4 minutes, 12 seconds
Additional producer: David Bowie
2. 'Having It All' performed by Eighth
Wonder
Words and music by Kensit,
Godson and Beauchamp
Time: 3 minutes, 6 seconds
3. 'Rodrigo Bay' performed by
Working Week
Words and music by Booth,
Stabbins and Roberts
Time: 3 minutes, 31 seconds
4. 'Selling Out' performed by Slim
Gaillard
Words and music by Taylor, Temple
and Gaillard
Time: 3 minutes, 37 seconds
5. 'Riot City' performed by Jerry
Dammers
Words and music by Jerry
Dammers
Time: 8 minutes, 29 seconds
Additional producer: Jerry
Dammers

ALBUM VARIATIONS

Diamond Life (European cassette
version)
*1. 'Snake Bite'
Music by Stuart Matthewman,
Andrew Hale and Paul S. Denman
Time: edited on to end of song
'Smooth Operator' to yield total of
7 minutes, 28 seconds
Producer: Robin Millar
*2. 'Love Affair with Life'
Words by Sade Adu; music by Sade
Adu and Ray St John
Time: 4 minutes, 35 seconds
Producer: Robin Millar
* These additional songs are not on
the album, nor are they on
American cassettes.

Promise (cassette and CD
versions)
1. 'You're Not the Man'
Words by Sade Adu; music by Sade
Adu and Stuart Matthewman
Time: not listed
Producers: Sade Adu, Stuart
Matthewman, Andrew Hale, Paul S.
Denman, Robin Millar and Ben
Rogan
2. 'Punch Drunk'
Music by Andrew Hale
Time: not listed
Producer: Robin Millar
Neither of these songs is on the
album.

SINGLES

(1) 'Hang on to Your Love' ('A' side)
Words by Sade Adu; music by Sade Adu and Stuart Matthewman
Time: 4 minutes, 19 seconds
Producer: Robin Millar
'Cherry Pie' ('B' side)
Words by Sade Adu; music by Sade Adu, Stuart Matthewman, Andrew Hale and Paul S. Denman
Time: 4 minutes, 25 seconds
Producer: Robin Millar

(2) 'Smooth Operator' ('A' side)
Words by Sade Adu; music by Sade Adu and Ray St John
Time: 4 minutes, 54 seconds
Producer: Robin Millar
'Spirit' ('B' side)
Words by Sade Adu; music by Sade Adu, Stuart Matthewman, Paul S. Denman and Ray St John
Time: 5 minutes, 28 seconds
Producer: Robin Millar

(3) 'Your Love Is King' ('A' side)
Words by Sade Adu; music by Sade Adu and Stuart Matthewman
Time: 3 minutes, 39 seconds
Producer: Robin Millar
'Love Affair with Life' ('B' side)
Words by Sade Adu; music by Sade Adu and Ray St John
Time: 4 minutes, 35 seconds
Producer: Robin Millar

(4) 'The Sweetest Taboo' ('A' side)
Words by Sade Adu; music by Sade Adu and Ray St John
Time: 4 minutes, 24 seconds
Producer: Robin Millar
'You're Not the Man' ('B' side)
Words by Sade Adu; music by Sade Adu and Stuart Matthewman
Time: 5 minutes, 9 seconds
Producers: Sade Adu, Stuart Matthewman, Andrew Hale, Paul S. Denman, Robin Millar and Ben Rogan

(5) 'Never as Good as the First Time' (remix edit) ('A' side)
Words by Sade Adu; music by Sade Adu and Stuart Matthewman
Remix by Ben Rogan, Mike Pela, Sade Adu, Stuart Matthewman, Paul S. Denman and Andrew Hale
Time: 3 minutes, 57 seconds
Producers: Mike Pela and Ben Rogan
'Keep Hanging On' (live instrumental) ('B' side)
Music by Sade Adu, Andrew Hale, Stuart Matthewman and Gordon Hunte
Remix by Ben Rogan, Mike Pela, Sade Adu, Stuart Matthewman, Paul S. Denman and Andrew Hale
Time: 2 minutes, 59 seconds
Producers: Mike Pela and Ben Rogan

12-INCH SINGLES AND EPS

(1) 'Hang on to Your Love' ('A' side) (American extended-play dance single)
Words by Sade Adu; music by Sade Adu and Stuart Matthewman
Time: 6 minutes
Producer: Robin Millar
'Hang on to Your Love' ('B' side) (short version)
Words by Sade Adu; music by Sade Adu and Stuart Matthewman
Time: 4 minutes, 19 seconds
Producer: Robin Millar

(2) 'Your Love Is King' ('A' side) (LP version/non-commercial 12-inch promotional single)
Words by Sade Adu; music by Sade Adu and Stuart Matthewman
Time: 3 minutes, 39 seconds
Producer: Robin Millar
'Your Love Is King' ('B' side) (short version)
Words by Sade Adu; music by Sade Adu and Stuart Matthewman
Time: 3 minutes, 28 seconds
Producer: Robin Millar

(3) 'The Sweetest Taboo' ('A' side) (extended version, British EP)
Words by Sade Adu; music by Sade Adu and Martin Ditcham
Time: 5 minutes, 30 seconds
Producer: Robin Millar
'You're Not the Man' ('B' side)
Words by Sade Adu; music by Sade Adu and Stuart Matthewman
Time: 5 minutes, 20 seconds
Producers: Sade Adu, Stuart Matthewman, Andrew Hale, Paul S. Denman, Robin Millar and Ben Rogan

(4) 'Is It a Crime?' ('A' side/cut no. 1) (British EP)
Words by Sade Adu; music by Sade Adu, Stuart Matthewman and Andrew Hale
Time: not listed
Producer: Robin Millar
'Wired' ('A' side/cut no. 2)
Music by Stuart Matthewman, Andrew Hale, Paul S. Denman, Martin Ditcham and Dave Early
Time: not listed
Producer: Robin Millar
'Punch Drunk' ('B' side)
Music by Andrew Hale
Time: not listed
Producer: Robin Millar

(5) 'Never as Good as the First Time' (extended remix) ('A' side)
Words by Sade Adu; music by Sade Adu and Stuart Matthewman
Remix by Ben Rogan, Mike Pela and Sade Adu
Time: 5 minutes, 12 seconds
Producers: Mike Pela and Ben Rogan
'Keep Hanging On' (live instrumental) ('B' side)
Music by Sade Adu, Andrew Hale, Stuart Matthewman and Gordon Hunte
Remix by Ben Rogan, Mike Pela, Sade Adu, Stuart Matthewman, Paul S. Denman and Andrew Hale
Time: 2 minutes, 59 seconds
Producers: Mike Pela and Ben Rogan

V I D E O G R A P H Y

MUSIC VIDEOS
(1) 'Hang on to Your Love'
Directors: B. Ward and K. Thorton
(2) 'Smooth Operator'
Director: Julien Temple
(3) 'Your Love Is King'
Director: Julien Temple
(4) 'When Am I Going to Make a Living?'
Director: Stuart Orme
(5) 'Sweetest Taboo'
Director: B. Ward
(6) 'Is It a Crime?'
Director: B. Ward

VIDEO-CASSETTES
(1) Diamond Life video by Sade
Released: July 1985
(CBS/Fox Video)
Contains four segments of interview
footage with Sade Adu speaking
about her life, her background and
her music; plus four video clips:
1. 'Hang on to Your Love'
Directors: B. Ward and K. Thorton
2. 'Smooth Operator'
(extended version)
Director: Julien Temple
3. 'Your Love Is King'
Director: Julien Temple
4. 'When Am I Going to Make a Living?'
Director: Stuart Orme

F I L M O G R A P H Y

(1) Absolute Beginners
(colour/1986)
Virgin and Goldcrest present a
  Palace Production
Director: Julien Temple
Producers: Stephen Woolley and
  Chris Brown
Writers: Richard Burridge,
  Christopher Wicking and Don
  MacPherson
Based on: *Absolute Beginners*, a
  novel by Colin MacInnes
Executive producers: Nik Powell,
  Robert Devereaux and Al Clark

Cast:

Colin......................Eddie O'Connell	Cool..........................Tony Hippolyte
Crêpe Suzette...............Patsy Kensit	Call Me Cobber........Alan Freeman
Vandice Partners.........David Bowie	Baby Boom........................Chris Pitt
Henley............................James Fox	Dean Swift........................Paul Rhys
Arthur............................Ray Davies	Misery Kid......................Julian Firth
Big Jill............................Eve Ferret	Hoplite........................Joe McKenna
The Fanatic...............Steven Berkoff	Amberley Drove........Ronald Fraser
Athene Duncannon...........Sade Adu	Mrs Larkin.................... Irene Handl
Dido Lament...............Anita Morris	Cynthia Eve....................Sylvia Syms
Harry Charms...............Lionel Blair	Salt Beef Man.................. Eric Sykes
The Wizard..Graham Fletcher Cook	Vern......................Peter Hugo Daly
Ma....................Mandy Rice-Davies	Saltzman...............Johnny Shannon
Flikker...........................Bruce Payne	Dorita.............Amanda Jane Powell
Ed the Ted.................Tenpole Tudor	Mario....................Robbie Coltrane

Includes music by Sade, David
Bowie, the Style Council, Ray
Davies and others.

C H R O N O L O G Y

16 January 1959 – Helen Folasade Adu born in Ibadan, Nigeria

1963 – Sade, her brother Banji and her mother Anne Adu leave her father in Nigeria and move to England

1970 – Sade's mother re-marries and the family moves to Clacton-on-Sea, Essex

1973 – Sade develops an interest in music and begins scouring record shops for Billie Holiday and Dinah Washington albums

1976 – Sade leaves home for London, where she begins attending St Martin's School of Art to study fashion design

May 1981 – Sade's menswear designs are displayed in New York City at the Axiom Show in conjunction with an appearance of the group Spandau Ballet. She makes her first trip across the Atlantic for the event

1981 – Sade is invited to audition for the 'funk' band Pride. She fails the initial audition but two weeks later the band-members change

their mind and Sade becomes a singer with Pride

1982 – The group 'Sade' makes its début at Ronnie Scott's jazz club in London

October 1983 – Sade signs a record deal with Epic Records in London

February 1984 – Sade's first single, 'Your Love Is King', is released in Britain

July 1984 – The *Diamond Life* album is released in Europe

13 July 1984 – Sade performs at the Montreux Jazz Festival, Switzerland

February 1985 – *Diamond Life* is awarded 'Best Album' prize by the BPI (British Phonographic Industry)

February 1985 – The *Diamond Life* album is released in the USA and Canada to instantaneous acceptance from record-buyers

May 1985 – *Diamond Life* is certified 'platinum' for selling one million copies in the USA and the 'Smooth Operator' single enters the Top Ten

13 July 1985 – Sade is one of the stars of the historic *Live Aid* concert, viewed by a billion and a half music fans worldwide via television satellite

July 1985 – The *Diamond Life* video-cassette is released

November 1985 – The *Promise* album is released and becomes an immediate worldwide hit

10-20 December 1985 – Sade's début American concert performances: 'The *Promise* Tour'

15 February 1986 (the week of) – *Promise* becomes the no. 1 album in the USA on the *Billboard* charts and sales exceed one million

25 February 1986 – Sade wins the 'Best New Artist' Grammy Award in the USA

March 1986 – The soundtrack album from the film *Absolute Beginners* is released

April 1986 – The film *Absolute Beginners* is premièred in London

Spring/summer 1986 – Sade world tour

SOURCES

Advertising Age; Beacon Journal, Akron, Ohio; *Billboard; Blues & Soul; Bop; Cash Box; Company; Cosmopolitan; Creem; Daily Mirror,* London; *East Village Eye; The Face; Friday Morning Quarterback; Herald-Mail,* Hagerstown, Maryland; *Hollywood Reporter; Jet; Los Angeles Times; Mademoiselle; Music Express; Musician; Music Track; Newsweek; New York Daily News; New York Post; New York Times; No. 1; People; Playboy; Pulse; Record; Rock & Soul; Rolling Stone; R.P.M. Weekly,* Toronto, Canada; *San Francisco Examiner; Seventeen; Spin; Star Hits; Sun,* Gainsville, Florida; *The Sunday Times,* London; *Time; US; USA Today; Vanity Fair; Video Business; Videofile; Village Voice; Vogue; VRS; 'W'.*